AFGHANISTAN AND THE ANGLO-RUSSIAN DISPUTE

AFGHANISTAN AND THE ANGLO-RUSSIAN DISPUTE

Theophilus Francis Rodenbough

A General Books LLC Publication.

Modifications Copyright ©2009 by General Books LLC. All rights reserved.

Published by General Books LLC.

You may not reproduce this book, stored it in a retrieval system, or transmitted in any form or by any means, electronic, mechanical, photocopying, recording, scanning, or otherwise, except as permitted under Section 107 or 108 of the 1976 United States Copyright Act, without either the prior written permission of the Publisher, or authorization through payment of the appropriate per-copy fee to the Copyright Clearance Center, Inc., 222 Rosewood Drive, Danvers, MA 01923, (978) 750-8400, fax (978) 646-8600, or on the web at www.copyright.com.

Limit of Liability/Disclaimer of Warranty: While the publisher and author have used their best efforts in preparing this book, they make no representations or warranties with respect to the accuracy or completeness of the contents of this book and specifically disclaim any implied warranties of merchantability or fitness for a particular purpose. No warranty may be created ore extended by sales representatives or written sales materials. The advice and strategies contained herin may not be suitable for your situation. You should consult with a professional where appropriate. Neither the publisher nor author shall be liable for any loss of profit or any other commercial damages, including but not limited to special, incidental, consequential, or other damages. Please keep in mind that this book was written long ago; the information in it is not current.

We have recreated this book from the original using Optical Character Recognition software to keep the cost of the book as low as possible. Therefore, could you please forgive any spelling mistakes, missing or extraneous characters that may have resulted from smudged or worn pages? When in doubt, please consult the original scanned book which may be available from our website.

For information on our books please go to www.general-books.net.

CONTENTS

1	Section 1	1
2	Section 2	5
3	Section 3	11
4	Section 4	27
5	Section 5	45
6	Section 6	57
7	Section 7	61

1

SECTION 1

LIST OF ILLUSTRATIONS.
MAPS.

Afghanistan and the Surrounding Territories (Drawn for this Work and Corrected by the Latest Military Surveys) . . *End of Vol.*
The Asiatic Territories Absorbed by Russia During the Past Two Centuries, with the Dates of the Various Annexations . . . I
The Russian Lines of Advance from their Base of Supplies . . 13
CUTS.
Abdurrahman Khan, Ameer of Kabul .... *Fronti'spicce.*
Mahaz Khan (A Tajik), Khan of Pest Bolak)
Jehandad (Lohanir), from Ghazni j 7
Wullie Mohammed, a Dahzungi Hazara)
Pozai Khan, a Shinwarri (Musician) j 19
Khan Baz, a Khumbhur Khel Afreedi)
Tooro Baz, a Kookie Khel Afreedi) 2I
Zool Kuddar, an Adam Khel Afreedi)
Mousa, a Kizilbash, Born in Peshawur ' ' ' ' ""'

Afghanistan and the Anglo-Russian dispute. Theophilus Francis Rodenbough

The City of Kandahar, Afghanistan 33
Castle of Zohak, First March from Bamian, Irak Road to Kabul . 37
An Afghan Post-Chaise ; Going to the Front 39
Gate of the Bazaar at Kabul 49
Major-General, Sir F. S. Roberts, V.C., K.C.B 57
Khelat-i-Ghilzi, between Kandahar and Ghazni 67
Elephant with Artillery ; on the Road to Alt Musjid ... 71
Detail of Elephant Saddle 75
Noah's Valley, Kunar River 81
Watch Tower in the Khaiber Pass 83
Fort of All Musjid, from the Heights above Lala Cheena, in the Khaiber Pass 85
Fort of Dakka, on the Kabul River 87
The Ishbola Tepc, Khaiber Pass 89
Entrance to the Bolan Pass, from Dadur 93
Entrance to the Khojak Pass, from Pishin, on the Road to Kandahar. 97
The Order of March in Central Asia 123
Gorge in the Tirband-i-Turkestan, through which the Murghab flows 125
Jelalabad, from Piper's Hill 127

AFGHANISTAN AND THE ANGLO-RUSSIAN DISPUTE.

THROUGH THE GATES OF ASIA.

In universal history there is no more interesting subject for the consideration of the political student than the record of Russian progress through Central Asia.

In one sense this advance is a practical reestablishment or extension of the influence of the Aryan race in countries long dominated by peoples of Turki or Mongolian origin; in another sense it has resulted in a transition from the barbarism or rude forms of Asiatic life to the enlightenment and higher moral development of a European age. In a religious sense it embodies a crusade against Oriental fanaticism ; and it is a curious feature of the Anglo-Russian dispute, that upon a question of temporal gain, the greatest Christian nation finds itself allied with the followers of Buddha and Mahomet against Russia under the Banner of the Cross.

The descendants of the great Peter have opened up in Central Asia a new region which, if as yet it has not been " made to blossom as the rose," has nevertheless profited by the introduction of law, order, and a certain amount of industrial prosperity.

Russia commenced her relations with Central Asia as early as the sixteenth century. Not only through embassies sent, but by military expeditions; these, however, at that time were private ventures by roving Cossacks and other inhabitants of Southern Russia. Authorized government expeditions commenced with Peter the Great, who in 1716-17 sent two exploring parties into the Central Asian deserts|Bekovitch to Khiva, and Likhareff to the Black Irtish. These expeditions were undertaken in search of gold, supposed to exist in those regions, but failed in their object; the detachment under Bekovitch being entirely destroyed after reaching Khiva. Peter next turned his attention to the country bordering upon the southern shores of the Caspian Sea;

taking advantage of Persian embarrassments, with the consent of the Shah and of the Sultan he acquired, in 1722-3, the provinces of Gilan, Mazanderan, and Asterabad; but the great expense of maintaining a large garrison so remote from Russia, and the unhealthiness of the locality, induced the Russian Government, in 1732, to restore the districts to Persia. In the same year Abul-Khair, the Khan of the Little Kirghiz Horde, voluntarily submitted to Russia. Twenty years later a small strip of the kingdom of Djungaria, on

2

SECTION 2

the Irtish, was absorbed, and toward the commencement of the reign of Catharine II., Russian authority was asserted and maintained over the broad tract from the Altai to the Caspian. This occupation was limited to a line of outposts along the Ural, the Irtish, and in the intervening district. During Catharine's reign the frontier nomads became reduced in numbers, by the departure from the steppe between the Ural and Volga of the Calmucks, who fled into Djungaria, and were nearly destroyed on the road, by the Kirghiz.

The connection between Russia and Central Asia at this time assumed another character, that of complete tranquillity, in consequence of the development of trade through Orenburg and to some extent through Troitsk and Petropaulovsk. The lines along the Ural and Irtish gradually acquired strength; the robber-raids into European Russia and Western Siberia almost entirely ceasing. The allegiance of the Kirghiz of the Little and Central Hordes was expressed in the fact that their Khans were always selected under Russian influence and from time to time appeared at St. Petersburg to render homage. With the Central Asian khanates there was no connection except that of trade, but as regarded the Turcomans, who, it is said, had frequently asked for Russian protection, intercourse was discouraged, as they could not be trusted "within the lines," being simply bandits.

The Emperor Paul imagined that the steppes offered a good road to Southern Asia, and desiring to expel theEnglish from India, in the year 1800 he despatched a large number of Don Cossacks, under Orloff, through the districts of the Little Horde. At the time a treaty was concluded with Napoleon, then First Consul, by virtue of which a combined Russo-French army was to disembark at Asterabad and march from thence into India by way of Khorassan and Afghanistan. The death of the Emperor of Russia put an end to this plan.

During the reign of Alexander I., Central Asia wa$ suffered to rest, and even the Chinese made raids into Russian territory without interruption. In the third decade of the present century, however, several advanced military settlements of Cossacks were founded. " Thus," says M. Veniukoff, " was inaugurated the policy which afterward guided us in the steppe, the foundation of advanced settlements and towns (at first forts, afterwards *stanitsas)* until the most advanced of them touches some natural barrier."

About 1840, it was discovered that the system of military colonization was more effectual in preserving order in the Orenburg district than by flying detachments sent, as occasion required, from Southern Russia; and in 1845-6 the Orenburg and Ural (or Targai and Irgiz) forts were established. In 1846 the Great Kirghiz Horde acknowledged its subjection to Russia on the farther side of the Balkash, while at the same time a fort was constructed on the lower Yaxartes.

Cossack settlements.

In 1847 the encroachments of Russia in Central Asia had brought her upon the borders of the important khanates of Khiva and Khokand, and, like some huge boa-constrictor, she prepared to swallow them. In 1852 the inevitable military expedition was followed by the customary permanent post. Another row of forts was planted on the Lower Yaxartes, and in 1854 far to the eastward, in the midst of the Great Horde, was built Fort Vernoyelthe foundation of a new line, more or less contiguous to natural boundaries (mountains and rivers), but not a close line. Between Perovsky and Vernoye there were upwards of four hundred and fifty miles of desert open to the incursions of brigands, and between the Aral and Caspian seas there was a gap, two hundred miles in width, favorable for raids into the Orenburg Steppe from the side of Khiva. Finally, under the pretext of closing this gap, a general convergent movement of the Siberian and Orenburg forces commenced, culminating under General Tchernayeff in the capture of Aulieata and Chemkent in 1864, and of Tashkent in 1865.

Here, M. Veniukoff says: " The Government intended to halt in its conquests, and, limiting itself to forming a closed line on the south of the Kirghiz steppes, left it to the sedentary inhabitants of Tashkent to form a separate khanate from the Khokand so hostile to us." And this historian tells us that the Tashkendees declined the honor of becoming the Czar's policemen in this way, evidently foreseeing the end, and, to cut the matter short,

i

chose the Russian general, Tchernayeff, as their Khan. The few Central Asian rulers.whose necks had so far escaped the Muscovite heel, made an ineffectual resistance, and in 1866 Hodjeni and Jizakh were duly "annexed," thus separating Bokhara and Khokand.

Here we may glance at the method by which Russia took firmer root on the shores of the Caspian, and established a commercial link with the Khivan region. In 1869 a military post and seaport was planted at Krasno- vodsk, on that point of the east shore of the Caspian, which presents the greatest facilities for shipping, and as a base of operations against the Turcomans, who were at that time very troublesome. Several military expeditions set out from this point, and every year detachments of troops were despatched to keep the roads open toward Khiva, the Kepet Dagh, or the banks of the Attrek. Within five years (i87O-'75) the nomads living within the routes named had become " good Turcomans," carried the Czar's mails to Khiva, and furnished the Krasno- vodsk-Khivan caravans with camels and drivers. But the colonization scheme on the lower Caspian had once more brought the Russians to the Persian boundary. In 1869 the Shah had been rather officiously assured that Russia would not think of going below the line of the Attrek; yet, as Colonel Veniukoff shows, she now regrets having committed herself, and urges'" geographical ignorance" of the locality when the assurance was given, and the fact that part of her restless subjects, on the Attrek, passeight months of the year in Russian territory and four in " so-called " Persia ; it is therefore not difficult to imagine the probable change on the map of that quarter.

The march continued toward Khiva, and after the usual iron-hand-in-velvet-glove introduction, General Kaufmann in 1873 pounced upon that important khanate, and thus added another to the jewels of the Empire. Nominally, Khiva is independent, but nevertheless collects and pays to Russia a considerable contribution annually.

In 1868 Russia seized Samarcand, and established over the khanate of Bokhara a similar supervision to that in Khiva. As the distinguished Russian already quoted remarks: " The programme of the political existence of Bokhara as a separate sovereignty was accorded to her by us in the shape of two treaties, in 1868 and 1873, which defined her subordinate relation to Russia. But no one looks at these acts as the treaties of an equal with an equal. They are instructions in a polite form, or programmes given by the civilized conqueror to the conquered barbarians, and the execution of which is guaranteed by the immediate presence of a military force."

The district of Khokand, whose ruler, Khudoyar Khan, submitted himself to Russia in 1867, was for a number of years nominally independent, but becoming disturbed by domestic dissensions, was ultimately annexed under the name of the Fergana Province.

To this point we have followed Colonel Vertiukoff's account of the Russian advance. It will doubtless interestthe reader to continue the narrative from an English view, exceptionally accurate and dispassionate in its nature.

In a lecture before the Royal United Service Institution in London, May 16, 1884, Lieut-General Sir Edward Hamley, of the British Army, discussed the Central Asian question before an audience comprising such Indian experts as Sir Henry Rawlinson, Lord Napier of Mag- dala, and Mr. Charles Marvin, and many distinguished officers, including Lord Chelmsford, Sir F. Haines, and Colonel Malleson. Among other things, General Hamley said:

" Probably England has never been quite free, during the present century, from some degree of anxiety caused by the steady, gradual approaches of Russia through Central Asia toward India. It was seen that where her foot was planted it never went back. It was seen that with forces comparatively small she never failed to effect

any conquest she was bent on, and that the conquest, once effected, was final. This security in possession was owing in great measure to the fact that the governments she displaced were bad governments, and that she substituted one far better in itself and of a simplicity which was well adapted to the people with whom she was dealing. She aimed mainly at three things|the establishment of order and of confidence and the obtaining of some return for her own heavy expenses. From the establishment of order and of confidence sprang a prosperity which en-
 abled her to obtain a certain revenue, though entirely inadequate to her expenditure. Thus we beheld her pressing solidly on, and we knew not where she might stop. Pretexts, such as it was difficult to find a flaw in, were never wanting on which to ground a fresh absorption of territory. And seeing behind this advance a vast country|almost a continent|which was not merely a great Asiatic Power, but a great European State, under autocratic, irresponsible rule, with interests touching ours at many points, it is not to be wondered at that we watched with anxiety her progress as she bore steadily down toward our Indian frontier."

General Hamley says that England became particularly suspicious of Russia in 1867 when she absorbed Turkestan, and this feeling was intensified in 1878, while the Treaty of Berlin was still pending. General Kaufmann assembled a small army of about 12,000 mefl and thirty- two guns on the frontier of Bokhara, and although upon the signing of the treaty all threatening movements ceased, yet the British commander then operating in Afghanistan knew that Kaufmann had proposed to march in the direction of Kabul, and menace the British frontier.

It has ever been the practice of Russia, in her schemes of aggrandizement, to combine her diplomatic with her military machinery; but, unlike other nations, the ambassador has generally been subordinate to the general.

At the time that General Kaufmann sheathed his sword under the influence of the Treaty of Berlin, in 1878, thereremained another representative of Russia|General Stolietoff|who had been quietly negotiating with the Ameer of Afghanistan, Shere AH, the terms of a " Russian treaty," whose characteristics have already been described. Hearing of this, the English Ambassador at St. Petersburg questioned the Russian Minister, who answered him "that no mission had been, nor was intended to be, sent to Kabul, either by the Imperial Government or by General Kaufmann." This denial was given on July 3d, the day after Stolietoff and his mission had started from Samarcand. After the envoy's arrival at Kabul, another remonstrance met with the reply that the mission was " of a professional nature and one of simple courtesy," and was not, therefore, inconsistent with the pacific assurances already given. The real nature of this mission became known from papers found by General Roberts at Kabul in 1879. These showed that Shere Ali had been invited to form a close alliance with the Russian Government. General Kaufmann had advised Shere Ali to try and stir up disaffection among the Queen's Indian subjects, promising to aid him, eventually, with troops. Finding that this scheme was impracticable at the moment, Russia dropped the Ameer, who fled from the scene of his misfortunes, and died soon after.

For the moment England breathed more freely. There were still great natural obstacles between the empires of Russia and of India. Not only the friendly state of Afghanistan, but on its northwestern border the neutral territory of Merv, hitherto an independent province, and inhabited by warlike tribes of Turcomans difficult to reach through their deserts and likely to harass a Russian advance to Herat to an embarrassing extent. It was seen that the possession of this territory would at once free Russia from much difficulty in case of an advance and give her the means of threatening Herat as well as Kabul from her base in Turkestan, and even to some extent to carry forward that base beyond the Oxus.

On the part of Russia, the success of General Skobeleff in capturing the fortified position of Geok Tp, January 24, 1880, marked the beginning of negotiations with the Turcomans for the acquisition of Merv. For a long while these were unsuccessful, but early in 1884 it was cabled to London, that " The Queen of the World " had accepted the White Czar as her future liege lord.

The immediate cause of this event was the effect produced upon the minds of the Turcoman deputation to Moscow by the spectacle of the Czar's coronation. The impression created by the gorgeous ceremonial was heightened by the presence of so many Asiatic chiefs and kinglets at the ancient and historic capital of Russia. The tales they brought back were well calculated to influence the minds of a wild and primitive people ; and when the Khan of Khiva proffered his services for the settlement of their relations with Russia, that section of the Tekke tribe in favor of peace accepted them. The chiefs tendered their formal submission to the Czar, and promised to allow Russian merchants to reside among them, andpledged themselves to maintain the security of the routes from the Oxus to the Tejend; also accepting the responsibilities of Russian subjects by rendering tribute either in money or by military service. To all intents and purposes it is equivalent to the establishment of a Russian garrison in Merv.

The thorough way in which Russia seeks to bind her Asiatic subjects is shown in the fact that in 1884, at the request of the Khan of Khiva, a Russian tutor was selected to instruct his children.

Soon after it was reported that the Russians had established themselves at Sarakhs on the direct road to Herat and just over the Persian boundary of Afghanistan. These later movements again aroused the distrust of England, and a joint commission of Russian and English officials was appointed early in the year 1885.

While the English members of the commission under Sir Peter Lumsden were awaiting the convenience of their foreign colleagues, the presence of Russian troops was reported on the disputed territory in the vicinity of Herat.

This action alarmed the Afghans, and a collision seemed imminent. The English Government considered M. de Giers' explanation of this encroachment unsatisfactory. Pending an adjustment of the new complication both nations prepared for the worst.

Here we will leave the subject of the Russian advance through the Gates of Asia and pass to the consideration of the present neutral ground of Afghanistan.

3

SECTION 3

II.
 ON THE THRESHOLD OF INDIA.
 From the Amu Daria and the Turcoman steppes to the deserts of Beloochistan, from Persian Khorassan to the valley of the Indus, stretches the country of the Afghans. Men of renown and events of world-wide interest have been connected with its history. Its records tell of the murder of Cavagnari in recent times; of the tragedy of Elphinstone's command (1838-42); of Shah Nadir, the butcher of Delhi (1738-39); of Baber Khan, the founder of Mongolian rule in India (1520); of Timur, the assailer of the world (1398); of Genghiz Khan, the annihilator of the civilization of ancient Asia (1218-24); of the great ruler, Sultan Mahmoud (a. D. 1000); and yet earlier, of Alexander, " the divinely favored Macedonian." Afghan history dies away, in the hymns of the Indian Vedas, eighteen hundred years before the birth of Christ.
 The territory of Afghanistan|which is destined to be the arena of a great international duel|covers an area of 12,000 square miles, or a tract measuring from north to south 688 miles, and from east to west 736 miles. It is a mountainous country; a high plateau, 6,000 feet above the sea, overlooked by lofty mountain ranges which open out and sink toward the west and south. On the north|it is bordered by the western ranges of the Himalayas, which reach to the Amu Daria; by the wall-like range of

Afghanistan and the Anglo-Russian dispute. Theophilus Francis Rodenbough 11 the Hindu Kush, some of whose peaks are 19,000 feet high ; and by several smaller ridges. Between the Kabul and Kuram rivers rises the snow-capped Sufeid Koh, the principal peak of which, to the south of Jelalabad, attains an altitude of 15,000 feet. To the south of this, in Southern Afghanistan, the Suleiman range, of an average height of 9,000 feet, falls rapidly toward the valley of the Indus. Between the Hindu Kush and the Suleiman ranges there are several lesser ones stretching toward the southwest, including the Auran Mountains (7,000 feet).

Of the principal rivers noted here (the Helmund, Har- i-Rud, Kabul, Kuram, and the Gomal) the Helmund alone is navigable. The Helmund terminates in the swamps of Seistan, as also do the Kash, Farrah, and Herat rivers, running parallel to the Helmund across the Kandahar-Herat roads, at 80, 150, and 200 miles, respectively, to the west of it. These rivers are without bridges, but (with the exception of the Helmund|provided with ferry at Girishk) are fordable, save in the months of April and May. The country is otherwise open and easily traversable, but only on the main routes can water be readily obtained, and forage is scarce in the winter.

The Turnuk valley, running northeast from Kandahar, is followed by the great route to Ghazni and Kabul skirting the Guikok range|separated from the Hazaristan to its west by the parallel valley of the Argandab. The latter valley is also followed by a route which enters it from Mooktur, the source of the Turnuk. This debouches upon the Herat road about ten miles west of Kandahar, and there is no communication west of it between Herat and Kabul, save by impracticable mountain routes across the Hazaristan.

Three routes from Kandahar to Herat separate at Girishk on the Helmund, cross the Kash at different points, and meet at Sabzawar (280 miles from Kandahar) on the Herat; both of the southernmost passing by the town of Farrah, which is 230 miles from Kandahar. From Girishk also a road follows the Helmund to Seistan and Lash Jowain, where it joins the Herat road at Farrah on the river of that name, or at Sabzawar on the Herat. The southernmost of the routes to Farrah also branches from Kash down the river named Kash, joining the Seistan route at Lash.

The general aspect of Afghanistan is that of a series of elevated flat-bottomed valleys, in the vicinity of the streams, somewhat under cultivation. The scenery is often wild and beautiful, and some of the defiles to the north of the Hindu Kush are said to be of appalling grandeur, while the soft, still loveliness of the sheltered glens on the southern slope of that range strongly impresses the traveller who visits them. Some of the ranges in the north and northeast are well timbered with pine and oak. The eastern half of Afghanistan is generally cold and rugged, but sustains innumerable flocks and herds, andabounds in mineral wealth, especially lead and sulphur. In the more sheltered valleys considerable fruit is grown, but only grain enough for the actual consumption of the inhabitants. Water and fodder abound, but fuel is deficient ; a serious matter, as the cold in the winter is extreme. The western part of Afghanistan is a more fertile region, interspersed, it is true, with lofty ranges, but comprising many pleasant valleys and pastures.

The population is approximately estimated at eight millions. Afghanistan is a genuine society of different nations, although the greater part are of Persian descent.

The strongholds of the German self-protecting federations are here produced on a large scale.

Thus the Duranis, Tajiks, Yusafzais, Ghilzais, Eimaks, Hazaris, Kaffirs, Hindus, Jats, Arabs, Kizilbashis, Uzbeks, Biluchis, are near neighbors; of these about 3,00x3,000 may be real Afghans who profess the Suni faith and speak Indo-Persian Puchtu. There are over four hundred inferior tribes known. The Duranis are numerically strongest and live in the vicinity of Kandahar. Next in importance are the Ghilzais, estimated at 30,000 fighting men living in the triangle|Kabul, Jelalabad, Khelat-i- Ghilzai; until 1747 they furnished the rulers of Afghanistan. To the south of the Ghilzais live the Puchtu- speaking races who chiefly defend only their own territory ; the mountainous eastern border is inhabited by the Momunds, Afridis, Arakzais, Zymukts, Waziris, who have never been subdued. Their sense of independence, however, does not prevent them from selling their friendship for ready money to the highest bidder. On the watershed of the Helmund and Indus dwell the independent Pathans and Biluchis. The Persian-speaking Kizilbashis in Kabul, comprise 3,000,000 of Shiahs, who are not Afghans, .many of whose 30,000 fighting men are in the Ameer's regular army. The Tajiks|about 10,000 men |are chiefly in the Kabul and Ghazni districts. The Hazaris and Eimaks are in the central section of Afghanistan, known as the Hazaristan, extending east and west from the Koushan pass over the Hindu-Kush range to Marchat on the Turcoman frontier, and north and south from Sirpool in Turkestan to Girishk, between Kandahar and Herat; they are the descendants of the military settlers left by the Tartar hordes that swept Central Asia under Genghiz Khan, and still maintain a quasi- independence ; they cordially detest the Afghan Government, but pay an annual tribute in money to its support. Finally there is a million of foreign nationalities, including Turks, Persians, Indians, Armenians, and Kaffirs; the last- named are Hindus, and violent antagonists of the Mohammedans living around them.

Thus it is seen that modern Afghanistan comprises three great districts|Herat in the west, Kabul in the east, and Kandahar in the centre, with the seat of government at the cities of the same names respectively. Within each district are, as already described, a large number of tribes occupying sub-districts, closely connected2 like the cells of a honey-comb, but each with its destinc- tive manners and customs and irregular military forces, in no instance numbering less than 6,000 men, and often twice that number, divided about equally into horse and foot. Many of these render military service to the Ameer, many are bandits in the worst sense. The nomadic tribes||like the Eimaks peopling the Heratic region||live principally in tents, encamping in winter in the valleys, and in summer on the table-lands of the mountain ranges. They are ignorant, hospitable, and brave and ardent hunters. Their principal trade is with Herat, and consists of woollen and camel-hair fabrics and clarified butter.

The farming population all live in small hamlets. The better classes of these live in villages surrounding or joined to the castle of a Khan. These castles are encompassed by a rude wall, having frequently turrets at the corners, and occasionally armed with swivel-guns or wall-pieces. The principal gardens are always on the outside of the castle, and the herds of horses and camels belonging to the Khan are kept at distant pastures and attended by herders, who live in tents. In the Bori and Ghazgar valleys the houses are of wood. In the Ghazgar valley they are all fortified, as already described ; the doors are generally mere man-holes, and the top of the towers are loopholes. The better class, and more modern of these, have flat roofs, from which the water is carried by spouts; the walls surrounding are at least twelve feet high, and cover

nearly an acre of ground. Three or four such houses usually constitute a village. These semi-barbarians are noted for the length and ferocity of their feuds. Sometimes two branches of a family who are neighbors become enemies. The distance between their " fortlets " may be two hundred yards, and on that space no one ventures. They go out at opposite gates and walk straight from their own fort in a line protected by its walls from the fire of the other, until out of range, then they turn around to their fields. Broadfoot relates that " once in Zurmat I saw a fort shut by rolling a stone against the door, instead of with the usual heavy chain. On inquiring as to the cause of such carelessness, the Malik, a fine old man with a plump, good-humored face, stretched his arms out toward the line of distant forts, and said: ' I have not an enemy!' It was a pleasing exception to the rule."

These feuds are a system of petty warfare, carried on by long shots, stealing cattle, and burning crops. Samson, burning his neighbor's corn, acted just like an Afghan. When the harvest is nearly ripe, neither party dare sleep. The remedy is sometimes for both to fight until an equal number are killed on each side, when the neighbors step in and effect a reconciliation ; another method is to pay forfeit of a feast and some sheep or cloth ; in exceptional cases, a few Afghan virgins are substituted for the sheep, but they are given in marriage, and are well treated.

Our space does not permit an extended reference to the manners and customs of this primitive people but afew characteristics may be briefly noted. The love of war is felt much more among Afghans than by other Eastern peoples, although but little effort has been made by them to augment the means of resistance and aggression. Pillage, fighting, and disturbances are at times necessary to their very existence, and are followed by long days of idleness, during which they live on the fruits of their depredations. There is no shade of difference between the character of the nomad and the citizen ; a town life does not soften their habits; they live there as they live in a tent, armed to the teeth and ready for the onslaught. Though full of duplicity, one is nevertheless liable to be taken in by their apparent frankness. They are hospitable to strangers, but only because this is an ancient custom which has the force of law and is not a virtue which springs from the heart. The pride of the Afghans is a marked feature of their national character. They boast of their descent, their prowess in arms, their independence ; and cap all by " Am I not a Puktan ?"

The Afghan people, occupied with the defence of their homes, have failed to assist the Ameer in the formation and maintenance of that indispensable instrumentIan organized, well-equipped, easily mobilized army. In regular battle the Afghans can have but little hope of success ; their strength lies in the petty warfare peculiar to a wild, mountainous country. As auxiliaries, as partisan troops in their own country, they would be of great value to their allies and extremely troublesome to their enemies.For outpost, courier, and scouting purposes, they would doubtless be most efficient. The strength of the organized army in the service of the Ameer of Afghanistan is about 50,000 men of all arms. The traveller Vambery, who visited Herat in 1863, says:

" The Afghan's national costume consists of a long shirt, drawers, and dirty linen clothes; or, if he is a soldier, he affects a British red coat. He throws it over his shirt, while he gets on his head the picturesque Indo- Afghan turban. Others againland these are the *beau- monde*lare wont to assume a half-Persian costume. Weapons are borne by all. Rarely does any one, whether civil or military, enter the bazar without his sword and shield. To be quite *ct la mode* one must carry about one quite an arsenal, consisting of two pistols, a sword, poniard, hand- jar, gun, and shield." M. Vambery also describes a drill of some Afghan regulars.

" The men had a very military bearing, far better than the Ottoman army that was so drilled forty years ago. These might have been mistaken for European troops if most of them had not had on their bare feet the pointed Kabuli shoe, and had not had their short trowsers so tightly stretched by their straps that they threatened every moment to burst and fly up above the knee."

The adventurous O'Donovan thus describes an Afghan cavalryman whom he met unexpectedly, near Herat, in 1880: " He wore a dark-colored turban, one end of the cloth pulled up in front so as to resemble a small cockade.

His uniform was blue-black, and he wore long boots. A broad black leather crossbelt, with two very large brass buckles, crossed his breast. He had sabre, pistols, and carbine."

The actual fighting strength of the army of Afghanistan cannot be definitely stated. Major Lumsden, who has represented the British Government in that country in various diplomatic capacities, stated (some years since) that the regular army of the Ameer consisted of sixteen regiments of infantry, three of cavalry, and seventy-six field guns. The infantry regiments numbered about 800 men each; the men were obtained by compulsory levy. Their uniform consisted of English cast-off clothes purchased at auction. The pay, about five rupees per mensem, was paid irregularly and often in kind ; two months' pay was deducted for clothing. The cavalry and artillery were badly horsed; and the horses were sent to graze in summer. A Russian report of 1868 estimates the infantry at 10,000 men. The armament, equipment, and instruction of the troops have doubtless improved since that time, as ten years later the British Government supplied the Afghan Government with 10,000 Enficld and 5,000 Snider rifles and one field battery, and very recently (1885) it was announced that a present of Martini-Henry rifles and improved field guns had been sent to Abdurrahman by the Indian authorities.

Besides the regular army there is a paid irregular mounted force of about 20,000 men, active and formidable in " hill operations," and known as Jezailchis.

The late General Colin Mackenzie, in an account of his experiences in the Elphinstone disaster of 1842, says:

"The Jezailchis are so called from their jezails or long rifles. The Afghans are said to be among the best marksmen in the world. They are accustomed to arms from early boyhood, live in a chronic state of warfare with their neighbors, and are most skilful in taking advantage of cover. An Afghan will throw himself flat, behind a stone barely big enough to cover his head, and scoop a hollow in the ground with his. left elbow as he loads. Men like these only require training to make first-rate irregular troops."

"As a trait of Afghan character, I must mention that whenever the Jezailchis could snatch five minutes to refresh themselves with a pipe, one of them would twang a sort of a rude guitar as an accompaniment to some martial song, which, mingling with the notes of war, sounded very strangely."

The Russian General Staff have also estimated the Ameer's force, exclusive of the irregulars, at 66,400 men with 30 guns.

The efficiency of this body, by reason of their peculiar surroundings, must vary with the character of the operations. For defence|particularly of their own section| they form an important consideration ; for aggressive purposes their strength lies in partisan operations, in small detachments, requiring great mobility.

Just as it is difficult to understand the rapidity withwhich large numbers are assembled in Afghanistan for fighting purposes, so the dispersing of an Afghan army together with its attendant masses of tribal levies in flight is almost beyond comprehension; men who have been actually engaged in hand-to-hand combat dispose of their arms in the villages they pass through, and meet their pursuers with melons or other fruit in their hands, while they adopt the *rdle* of peaceful inhabitants.

A brief description of some of the more noted cities of Afghanistan may be appropriate here.

Sir Henry Rawlinson gives the following details respecting the so-called Key of India|the city of Herat:

" That which distinguishes Herat from all other Oriental cities, and at the same time constitutes its main defence, is the stupendous character of the earthwork upon which the city wall is built. This earthwork averages 250 feet in width at the base and about 50 feet in height, and as it is crowned by a wall 25 feet high and 14 feet thick at the base, supported by about 150 semicircular towers, and is further protected by a ditch 45 feet in width and 16 feet in depth, it presents an appearance of imposing strength. Whether the place is really as strong as it looks has been differently estimated. General Fer- rier, who resided for some time in Herat, in 1846, states that the city is nothing more than an immense redoubt, and gives it as his opinion that, as the line of wall is entirely without flanking defences, the place could not hold out for twenty days against a European army; and M.Khanikoff, who, although not a professional soldier, was a very acute observer, further remarks that the whole interior of the city is dominated from the rising ground 700 yards distant and covered with solid buildings at the northeast angle, while the water supply both for the ditch and the city would be at the mercy of an enemy holding the outside country ; the wells and reservoirs inside the wall, which could then alone be available|being quite inadequate to the wants of the inhabitants: but on the other hand, all experience testifies to the defensibility of the position.

" Not to speak of the siege which Herat sustained at the hands of Genghiz Khan, of Timur, and of Ahmed Shah, we have only to remember that in 1837 the Afghans of Herat, under Major Eldred Pottinger, beat off the continuous attacks, for nearly ten months, of a Persian army of 35,000 regular troops supported by fifty pieces of artillery, and in many cases directed and even commanded by Russian officers. The truth seems to be that Herat, although in its present state quite unfit to resist a European army, possesses great capabilities of defence, and might by a skilful adaptation of the resources of modern science be made almost impregnable. Major Saunders, a British engineer officer, calculated in 1840 that, at an outlay of "60,000, which would include the expenses of deepening the ditch, clearing the glacis and esplanade, providing flanking defences, and repairing the walls throughout, Herat might be rendered secure against any possible renewal of the attack by Persia."

The location of this city upon the principal thoroughfare between India, Persia, and Turkestan gives it a special importance in a military sense. It is also the principal mart of Western Afghanistan, and comprises extensive manufactures in wool and leather. The natural fertility of the country near Herat has been enhanced by irrigation.

" The valley, *or jtilgah* (as the Persians say), in which the city lies is rich in the possession of a river. This valley is about thirty miles long by sixteen in breadth, exclusive of the ground taken up by the fortress and the walls. Four of these miles separate the town from the northern and twelve from the southern hills, while at one quarter of the greater distance runs the Her-i-Rud or Herat River, which, rising near the Kuh-i-Baba, pursues a westerly course till, passing the city, it sweeps, first gradually, then decidedly, to the north, eventually to lose its identity in the environs of Sarakhs. It is of political as well as of geographical importance, for it passes between the Persian and Afghan frontier posts of Kahriz and Kusun respectively, and may be considered to mark the Perso- Afghan boundary at the Western Paropismus. The Plain, south of the walls, is watered by a net-work of eight or nine large and many minor ditches. The aqueducts are stated to be superior to those of Bokhara, Samarcand, and Ispahan. The grain produced is abundantlbeyond the requirements of town and suburbs together. The bread, the water, and the vines have the merit of special excellence. Yet, with all this wealth of means and material, capable of subsisting an army of 150,000 men for some time, much of the legacy of past ages is disregarded and nullified by the supineness of a present generation. The ruins visible on all sides are not all useless or obsolete works. As one conclusive instance may be cited the neglected ' Pul-i-Malan.' This bridge, of twenty-three arches, can scarcely be considered void of purpose or practical benefit. It is, however, rapidly falling into decay, and as the river has changed its bed, part of it remains, barren of object, on dry land. On the rising of the waters this state of things is inconvenient ; for the river, at such time, is no longer fordable, and the Kandahar caravans, going to and fro, have difficulty in crossing."

In 1830 Conolly was of opinion that the city was one of the dirtiest in the world, being absolutely destitute of drainage; and Vambery, thirty-three years afterward, when the city was captured by Dost Mohammed, says the city was largely a heap of rubbish, having suffered the horrors of a long siege.

The city of Kabul, from which the surrounding territory of Eastern Afghanistan takes its name, stands in lat. 34 30' N., and long. 69 6' E., near the point where the Kabul River is crossed by three bridges. Its altitude is 6,400 feet, and, within a short distance to the north, is overtopped by pinnacles of the Hindu Kush about 14,000 feet higher.

Sir F. J. Goldsmid, " Journeys Between Herat and Khiva."

The winters are severe, but the summers are very temperatelseldom going above 80. Kabul is fortified without and within ; being separated into quarters by stone walls: the Bala Hissar, or citadel proper, being on the east, while the Persian quarter of the city is strongly protected on the southwest. In the days of Sultan Baber, Kabul was the capital of the Mogul empire. In modern times, it has been the scene of many Anglo- Indian struggles. It was taken by the British in 1839, and lost by them, through treachery, in 1841 ; in the following January, 4,000 British soldiers and 12,000 camp-followers were massacred while retreating.

Kandahar, the capital of Central Afghanistan, is about two hundred miles S. W. of Kabul, and three hundred and seventy-one miles E. of Herat. It is said to have been founded by Alexander of Macedon. The city is laid out at right angles, and is watered from the neighboring rivers through canals, which send to every street an ample supply. Sir Michael Biddulph describes the surroundings: " Kandahar stands on the western side of a plain, which was originally a barren skirt of the mountain. Exactly opposite to the city, and two miles to the westward, there is a wide break in the dividing ridge, through which the road to Herat leads, and by which are conducted the many canals and watercourses, taken from the Argandab, to supply the town and fertilize its environs. The energy and skill displayed in these extensive water-works cannot be too highly extolled. Brought from a point many miles

distant in the Argandab valley, the chief canal, with its offshoots, conducts a vast body of water, which is dispersed along the contours of the declining plain in innumerable channels, spreading a rich fertility for many miles in a fan-like form to the southeast of the gap. Villages cluster around the city on three sides ; cornfields, orchards, gardens, and vineyards are seen in luxurious succession, presenting a veritable oasis within the girdle of rugged hills and desert wastes all around. And if we turn to the aspect of the country beyond the gap, we see in the Argandab valley, along the canals and the river banks, a fair and beautiful landscape of village and cultivated ground, stretching for many miles in each direction. This productive character of the immediate neighborhood of Kandahar, and its commanding position within reach of other fertile districts, would give to this place, under a strong, stable, and just government, as much prosperity and happiness as falls to the lot of any place in the world."

Jelalabad stands on the Kabul River, about half-way between Kabul and the Khaiber Pass. It was the scene of the stubborn defence by Sir Robert Sale in 1842, referred to elsewhere. It has a floating population of about three thousand souls. Our engraving is taken from the south and west. The.stream in the west is the Kabul River. The Jati gate in the south wall is the exit from the Hindu quarter. The Kabul exit is on the west, while the road to Peshawur commences at the gate of that name on the east wall ofthe city. The northern gate is known as the Pheel Khana, or elephant quarter. The walls of the town and of its houses are of mud, and the roofs generally of wood. The city is laid out in the form of a parallelogram intersected by two main streets crossing in the centre.

The town of Ghazni (the ancient Ghizni) is another historical landmark in a region famous for its evidences of former grandeur. It stands about 230 miles northeast of Kandahar on the road to Kabul; it is literally " founded upon a rock " at an elevation of 7,726 feet, and its base is 280 feet above the adjacent plain. It has walls thirty-five feet high, and a wet ditch, but is not considered in any sense formidable by modern engineers, as it is commanded by neighboring heights ; it will always be a rendezvous for the natives, and forms a station or an important line of communication between the Indus and the Murghab. In the tenth century it was the seat of an empire comprising the present territory of Afghanistan, and which had in the space of seventy years absorbed thirty-eight degrees of longitude and twenty degrees of latitude. Its decline dates from the twelfth century, when the seat of government was transferred to Lahore. From 1839 to 1880 it has been occupied alternately by the British and the Afghans. The climate is not exceptionally severe, although in winter the mercury drops to 25 below zero at times. The population averages about ten thousand.

Peshawur is one of the most important towns, both in a military and commercial sense, in the *Derajat*. It is the capital of a province of the same name on the N. W. frontier of India, eighteen miles from the Khaiber Pass and one hundred and fifty miles S. E. of Kabul. It has the usual bastioned defences, besides some detached works of more importance. It was once a rich and populous city, but has, like many other like places in that region, fallen from its high estate. It is garrisoned by the British, and can boast of fair trade and a population of about fifty thousand. It is the centre of a fruitful district containing more than one million inhabitants.

The fruitful valley and pass of Bamian lie on the road leading from Kabul to Turkestan. The pass, at an elevation of 8,496 feet, is the only known defile over the Hindu Kush practicable for artillery. This valley was one of the chief centres of Buddhist worship, as gigantic idols, mutilated indeed by fanatical Mussulmans, conclusively prove. Bamian, with its colossal statues cut out in the rock, was among the wonders described by the Buddhist monks who traversed Central Asia in the fourth century. The statues are found on a hill about three hundred feet high, in which are a number of cells excavated in the rock, not unlike those found in the Zuni country in the western part of the United States. The male figure is about 160 feet, the female 120 feet, in height; they are clothed in light drapery, and a winding stair may be ascended to the head.

Eight miles eastward of Bamian lies the ancient fortress of Zohak, attributed to the fabulous Persian serpent-king of that name. It is still used as one of the defences of the pass.

The animals of Afghanistan adapted to military transport purposes are the camel, the *yabu* (mountain pony), and the donkey.

From certain professional papers, on the camel, by Captain Yaldwyn and other officers of the Indian Army, we learn that this beast of burden has been often utilized by the British in Afghanistan, and the supply of camels raised in that country has generally been augmented by drafts from India, although the last mentioned do not thrive under the transition. The camel is docile, capable of abstinence in an emergency, well adapted for the imposition of loads and for traversing over flat or sandy ground, adapts itself to rough roads, has acute sight and smell, and, during progression, moves both feet on one side, simultaneously. Its flesh and milk are wholesome articles of food. It is deficient in muscular power behind, and cannot readily climb hills. Those found in Afghanistan are of the Arabian species. They are strong, thickset, with abundance of hair; are short in the leg, better climbers, and more accustomed to cold than others of the species. Their feeding requires as much care as that of cavalry or artillery horses; they are fond of green food, and certain trees and shrubs. In grazing, camels brought from India sometimes are poisoned by eating the oleander bush and other plants which the native camel avoids. Elphinstone's ill-fated expedition in 1841 lost 800 out of 2,500 camels from this cause alone. On the march, or where grazing does not abound, they are fed with grain

and *bhoosa* ; this is given them in one ration at the end of the day. The theory that camels do not require much watering is declared a fallacy; the Arabian species can take in five or six gallons, sufficient for as many days ; they will not drink cold running water ; but, where water can be had, they should be watered daily. The load of the camel varies from 300 to 450 pounds, depending upon its condition. It is admirably adapted for carrying long articles, as ladders, tent-poles, and even light mountain guns. The marching power of camels depends on a number of conditions. They are good goers in loose sandy soil, and even over stony ground, if the stones are not too large and sharp ; in slippery places they are useless, as they have no hold with their feet. They are very enduring, making the longest marches at an average speed of two miles an hour, and can ford deep rivers with ease if the current is not too rapid. When the bottom of the ford is shifting sand, the passage of a number of camels renders it firm. A string of 50x3 camels covers about one mile of road ; 1,250 mules, carrying the same weight of supplies, occupy double the distance. Camels must be unladen at ferries. For military purposes these animals are purchased between the ages of five and nine years, and may be used up to the age of sixteen. They average about one thousand pounds in weight, seven feet in height to the top of the hump, and eight feet in length from nose to tail. In camp and when not at work they are arrangedin lines facing each other, or in circles heads inward ; the latter plan is the favorite formation at night. The allowance of spare camels on service is ten per cent.

Chopped straw.

Lieut. Martin, R. E., states that his company, of Sappers and Miners, was able to get an exceptional percentage of labor from the camels under his charge by attention to certain details; and says further, that " camels are very quarrelsome and bite each other badly when grazing. They can ford four feet of moderately running water, easily, if the bed is good ; but a yard of greasy mud, a few inches deep, will throw many camels and delay a convoy for hours. Camel-bridges were carried on the leading camels, with a few shovels and picks, in every convoy of the Kandahar Field Force, and all small cuts or obstructions were thus bridged in a few minutes ; the camels remaining by their bridges (two gang-boards eight by three feet) until the last baggage camel had passed. In perfectly open country, such as Kandahar to Girishk, it was found possible to march the camels on a broad front, the whole convoy being a rough square ; camels starting at 3 A.M. have been known to arrive at camp ten miles off as late as 5 P.M."

Captain Yaldwyn says: " A camel's carrying-power is equal to that of two and a half mules or ponies, whilst his ration is only about that of one mule or pony. Thus 500 camels only eat as much as 500 mules or ponies, and whilst the latter can only carry 1,000 *maunds* theformer can carry 2,500. Again, 500 camels only require 125 attendants to be paid, clothed, and fed, whilst 500 mules or ponies require 167 attendants." But, on the other hand, the immense losses of camels from excessive heat or cold, or over-exertion in mountainous or rough roads, and other causes, greatly neutralize the force of this comparison.

A *maunds* 80 pounds.

The *yabu* is a hardy mountain pony used by the Afghans for the saddle and packing purposes; they are very strong, active, and sure-footed, and have been frequently used by the British forces in their military operations. In 1839 Captain (afterward General) Outram relates that his *yabu*, " although but thirteen hands high, carried me and my saddlebags, weighing altogether upward of sixteen stone, the whole distance from Kalat in seven days and a half (an average of nearly forty-seven miles a day), during which time I had passed 111 hours on its back ; there was no saddle on the pony, merely a cloth over his back."

. They will carry from four to five maunds with perfect ease, making journeys of thirty miles a day. Those which are ridden and which amble, are called *yurgas.* The Afghans tie a knot in the middle of the long tails of their horses, which, they say, strengthens the animal's backbone !

The Afghan donkey was severely tested in 1880 during the operations of Sir Donald Stewart between Kabul and Kandahar, and this class of carriage was found very usefulin the conveyance of provisions. Afghan donkeys will march with troops and carry loads of grain or flour, averaging ninety pounds, without difficulty. They keep pace with mules or ponies in a baggage column, as they avoid the frequent checks which retard the larger animals; they browse on the line of march, and find their own forage easily in the neighborhood of camp ; they are easily controlled and cared for, and are on all accounts the most inexpensive transport in Eastern countries.

The transport animals found in India and Turkestan will be described in the parts of this book devoted to the military resources of those regions.

In concluding this sketch of the " Threshold of India," a mere glance at the military history of the country will suffice. In fact, only so far as it may have a bearing upon the present, has reference to the past any place in this volume.

The early periods of eventful interest to Afghanistan have been already noted at the opening of this chapter. Its purely Oriental experiences were beginning to fade with the death of Nadir Shah|variously termed the " Butcher of Delhi," and the " Wallace of Persia," in 1747. His progress toward India, from which he was to tear its choicest treasure and loot its greatest city, reminds one of the Arabian Nights. A camp-follower from Jelalabad reported as follows: " He has 36,00x3 horsemen with himself After morning prayers he sits on a throne,the canopy of which is in the form of a dome and of gold. One thousand young men, with royal standards of red silk and the lance tops and tassels of silver, are disposed regularly ; and, at a proper distance, five hundred beautiful slaves, from twelve to twenty years old, stand|one half on his right and the other on his left. All the great men stand fronting him; and the Arzb$gi stands between, in readiness to represent whatever he is desired, and everybody has his cause decided at once : bribery is not so much as known here. He has particular information given him of every thing that passes; all criminals, great and small, rich and poor, meet with immediate death. He sits till noon, after which he dines, then reposes a little ; when afternoon prayers are over he sits till the evening prayers, and when they are over he shoots five arrows into the *Khak Ttidah,* and then goes into the women's apartments."

Lieut.-Col. E. F. Chapman, C.B., R.A.

The splendor of the Robber King has departed, but his deeds of blood and treachery have often been repeated in the country of the Afghans.

A succession of struggles between Afghan and Persian leaders for the control of Afghanistan marked the next fifty years.

When the project of Russian invasion of India, suggested by Napoleon, was under consideration in Persia, a British envoy was sent, in 1809, to the then Shah Sujah, and received the most cordial reception at Peshawur. But Shah Sujah was, in 1810, superseded by his brother, Mahmud, and the latter was pressed hard by the son of his Wazir to such an extent that Herat alone remained to him. In 1823 his former kingdom passed to Dost Mohammed, who in 1826 governed Kabul, Kandahar, Ghazni, and Peshawur. The last-named place fell into the hands of Runjeet Singh, the " Lion of the Punjab." Dost Mohammed then applied to England for aid in recovering Peshawur, failing in which he threatened to turn to Russia.

Fraser's " Nadir Shah."

That Power was (1837) engaged in fomenting trouble in the western part of Afghanistan, encouraging an attack by 30,0x30 Persians, led by Russian officers, upon Herat. Instead of acceding to the request of Dost Mohammed, the British Governor-General|Lord Auckland|declared war against that potentate, alleging in a proclamation that " the welfare of the English possessions in the East rendered it necessary to have an ally on their western frontier who would be in favor of peace, and opposed to all disorders and innovations."

This was the beginning of intrigues relating to Afghanistan on the part, alternately, of England and Russia, in which John Bull has had to pay, literally, " the lion's share" of the cost in blood and treasure. In 1850, Sir John Cam Hobhouse, President of the Board of Control in India confessed : " The Afghan war *was done by myself;* the Court of Directors had nothing to do with it." The reason already mentioned was alleged as an excuse for hostilities. They were declared, notwithstanding that the British political agent at the Court of Dost Mohammed reported that ruler as " entirely English" in his sympathies. This report was suppressed. Twenty years later the facts were given to Parliament, Russian letters were found implicating the Czar's ministers, and the English agent, Burnes, was vindicated.

The Anglo-Indian army|consisting of twenty thousand troops, fifty thousand followers, and sixty thousand camels|advanced in two columns, one from Bengal, and the other from Bombay by 'the Indus. Scinde, which had hitherto been independent, like the Punjab and Lahore, was subjugated *en route,* and nine thousand men were left behind to occupy it. On the 23d of February, 1839, a simultaneous advance from Shikarpur, on the Bolan Pass, commenced. Kandahar was occupied April 25th, Ghazni July 23d, and Kabul August 6th, and Shah Sujah was proclaimed Ameer by British authority. By the following September the greater part of the English forces returned to India. Only five regiments of infantry and one of cavalry remained in Afghanistan, where suspicious symptoms of discontent with the new order of things began very soon to show themselves. During the summer of 1840 insurrections had to be put down by force in several places. In November of the same year Dost Mohammed defeated the English in the Perwan Pass. From that time until the autumn of 1841 a sultry calm reigned in the country.

The English commanders, although fully aware of the state of mind of the people, neglected to take the most simple measures of precaution.

The local control was vested in a mixed military and civil council, consisting of General Elphinstone, unfitted by disease and natural irresolution from exercising the functions of command, and *Sit* William McNaghten, the British envoy, whose self-confidence and. trust in the treacherous natives made him an easy victim. In the centre of an insurrection which was extending day by day under their eyes and under their own roofs, these representatives of a powerful nation, with a small but effective force, deliberately buried their heads in the sand of their credulity, not realizing the nature of the danger which for weeks was evident to many of their subordinates.

Finally a force of the insurgents, under the direction of the son of the deposed ruler, Akbar Khan, threw off the disguise they had assumed before the English, and taking possession of the Khurd Kabul Pass near the city, entirely cut off the retreat to India which Elphinstone had commenced.

As there was no intelligent concert of action among the British leaders, the garrison melted away in detail, the Afghan auxiliaries refused to fight, or turned their arms 'against the Europeans. Sir William McNaghten was murdered by Akbar, at a council in sight of the garrison. A few attempts to force a passage, or to defend themselves, made by certain brave officers of the beleagured force, failed.

On January 6, 1842, an agreement was made by which the Afghan leader promised to ensure to the British forces a safe withdrawal to India. This was violated with Afghan readiness, and the entire Anglo-Indian contingent of seventeen thousand souls was destroyed; sacrificed to the murderous brutality of the Afghan insurgents, or dying from exposure to one of the most severe winters known to that region. Months after, heaps of dead bodies, preserved by the intense cold, obstructed the mountain passes. The horrors of Moscow were repeated in the Khurd Kabul, and the noblest attributes of humanity were exemplified in the acts of the officers and soldiers of the doomed party. Only twenty of this entire force survived. The news of this horrible disaster was brought to Jelalabad by the only man who penetrated the Afghan environment, Dr. Brydon.

On receipt of the news of this overwhelming catastrophe, the Indian Government endeavored to rescue the garrisons of Kandahar and Ghazni, as well as that of Jelalabad; but the Mohammedan troops refused to march against their co-religionists, and the Sikhs also showed great unwillingness. The garrison of Ghazni, thinking to secure its safety by capitulation, was cut to pieces December 23, 1841. Jelalabad, held by 2,400 men under General Sale, still withstood the storm like a rock of iron. General Nott, the energetic officer commanding at Kandahar, on receiving the news of the destruction of the British, blew up the citadel of the town,

destroyed every thing not necessary to his object, and started, August 8, 1842, for Ghazni, which he also destroyed, September 6th.

Another British force of twelve thousand men, under General Pollock, was organized at Peshawur, to punish the Afghans, and, so far as might be, retrieve the errors of Elphinstone and McNaghten. Pollock's operations were, in the sense of retaliation, successful. An eminent German authority wrote : " Kabul and other towns were levelled with the ground; Akbar's troops were blown from guns, and the people were collected together and destroyed like worms." General Pollock carried the famous Khaiber Pass, in advancing to the relief of Jelalabad in April, 1842. This was the first time that the great defile |twenty-eight miles in length|had ever been forced by arms. Timur Lang and Nadir Shah, at the head of their enormous hosts, bought a safe passage through it from the Afridis. Akbar the Great, in 1587, is said to have lost forty thousand men in attempting to force it, and Aurang- zeb failed to get through.

The misfortune of Elphinstone's command, great as it was, would have been much more humiliating to England, had it not been for the firmness of the gallant General Pollock, who, ordered to withdraw with his command to Peshawur, by Lord Ellenborough, without effecting one of the objects of the expedition|the deliverance of the English captives in Akbar's hands at Kabul,|protested against such a suicidal act on the part of any Englishman or any Administration, and, at great personal risk, gained his point.

In the forced march to Kabul, which Pollock made subsequently, the force of about eight thousand men moved in as light order as possible. After loading the commissariat camels to their utmost carrying capacity, the General discovered that the mounted men had in their kit a spare pair of pantaloons apiece, on which he ordered the legs to be filled with grain and carried by the men in front of them, on their saddles. By the middle of December the British had started on their return march, pursued as far as the Indus by the Afghans, and by this hurried conclusion to the war lessened their prestige in Asia to an enormous degree.

As Sir Henry Rawlinson wrote:

" It was not so much the fact of our retreat; disaster would have been diminished, if not altogether overcome ; but retreating as we did, pursued even through the last pass into the plains by an implacable enemy, the impression became universal in India as well as in Central Asia, that we had simply been driven back across the mountains."

A very able Hindu gentleman, very loyal to the British, traced the mutiny of 1857 in a grea.t measure to the Afghan campaign of 1842. He said: " It was a direct breach of faith to take the Sepoys out of India. Practically they were compelled to go for fear of being treated as mutineers, but the double pay they received by no means compensated them for losing caste. The Sepoys mistrusted the Government from that time forward, and were always fearing that their caste would be destroyed ; besides, the Kabul disaster taught them that Europeans were not invincible."

The departure of the English forces was followed by the reestablishment of Dost Mohammed's authority in Afghanistan. Once, at the time of the Sikh insurrection, the Dost crossed the Indian border with two thousand horsemen, and narrowly escaped falling into the hands of the British in the affair of Gujrat, February 21, 1849, where the speed of his horse alone saved him from capture. In 1855 a better understanding was effected between the son of Dost Mohammed and his powerful European neighbor. He reconquered Balkh in 1850, and gained Kandahar by inheritance in 1855, while he lost Herat to the Persians in 1856. With the aid of Great Britain, in 1857, Persia relinquished all claims to Herat, but the Dost had eventually to besiege that city, occupied by a rebellious faction, in 1863, and after a siege of ten months reduced the place, only to find a tomb within its walls. After the usual struggle for the throne, peculiar to a change of dynasty in Afghanistan, Shere Ali, one of the Dost's sons, prevailed, and was recognized in 1868. The next decade was notable for a series of diplomatic manceu- vres between England and Russia for Afghan friendship. Shere Ali now leaned toward the Lion, now in the direction of the Bear, with the regularity of a pendulum. Theadvances were received with presents and promises on the one hand, and promises, powerful embassies, and imposing military expeditions on the other. On September 21, 1878, a British ambassador was turned back by the Afghan commandant of the frontier fort of Ali Musjid, and on the 2oth of November, of the same year, war was declared against Shere Ali by the Anglo-Indian Government. At that time the Russian General Kaufmann was operating on the northern border of Afghanistan with a force of fifteen thousand men and sixty guns, and the Ameer had reason to think that he could rely on Russian cooperation against the English, who, with a force of forty thousand men, promptly invaded his dominion.

This force moved into Afghanistan in four columns, under the command, respec- tively, of Generals Browne, Roberts, Biddulph, and Stewart, with reserves under Generals Maude and Primrose.

We shall have occasion later to consider some of the details of the protracted operations which followed. They embraced several admirably conducted marches, exposure to excessively severe winter weather, the successful surmounting of great nat- ural obstacles, the development of the usual weakness in the department of transport, with unnecessary losses in animals, a considerable sick-list, and an inconsiderable proportion of killed and wounded in action.

The military benefits were those resulting from a long and arduous field experience in a rough country. Theinterruption to these actual " field manoeuvres," this " fire- drill," by the enemy, was comparatively feeble,|as a rule, stimulating the Anglo-Indian force to put its best foot foremost. Under this system, at the end of the two years' campaign, all departments of the army had become moulded into the efficient machines essential to success in any military venture.

Politically, the campaign had been a failure. The fate of the gallant Major Cavagnari and his mission, murdered at Kabul, September 3, 1879, made a deeper impression on the Afghan mind than the British occupation of Afghan cities or the Afghan losses in battle.

In the same year the British Secretary for India, in London, wrote to the Governor- General that: " It appears that as the result of two successful campaigns, of the employment of an immense force, and of the expenditure of large sums of money, all that has yet been accomplished has been the disintegration of the State which it was desired to see strong, friendly, and independent, the assumption of fresh and unwelcome liabilities in regard to one of its provinces, and a condition of anarchy throughout the remainder of the country."

Early in the year 1880, the British Government prepared to make a dignified with- drawal from Afghanistan. That volcanic region was by no means tranquil, although the chief rebel, Yakoub Khan, had been driven out of Kabul by General Roberts, and had retired to the distant country of the Heri-i-rud. At this time appeared theexiled Ab- durrahman Khan, who had long resided at Tashkend, and who was welcomed warmly by the local sirdars on the northern frontier of Afghanistan. As he approached Kabul his authority and influence increased, and the British political officers, acting under instructions, formally recognized him as Ameer of that district. In the meanwhile Yakoub advanced westward from Herat with a strong force, encountered a British brigade, under General Burrows, near the Helmund, and utterly routed it. The remnant of the European force took refuge in Kandahar, where General Primrose was in command. Surrounding the city, Yakoub succeeded in effectually "bottling up" the British garrison for some time. Sir Frederick Roberts, however, made a rapid march from Kabul on Kandahar, and after a successful and decisive battle with the Afghans, completely dispersed the native force, and relieved the beleaguered garrison. Soon after, Abdurrahman was formally installed as Ameer of Afghanistan, and the British army withdrew from the country.

4

SECTION 4

III.
  THE BRITISH FORCES AND ROUTES.
  A SKETCH of the military resources of Great Britain, more especially those available for field service in Afghanistan, with notes upon the strength and composition of the forces, means of transport and supply, nature of important lines of communication, and of certain strategic points in the probable theatre of operations, will be attempted in this chapter.
  Organisation.|The military system of Great Britain is based upon voluntary enlistment instead of the usual European plan of universal liability to service. Recruits may enlist either for the " short-service " or " long-service" term ; the first being for six years in the ranks and six on furlough, and the last for twelve years in the ranks; the furlough of short-service men is passed in the army reserve, and then, in consideration of liability to be recalled to the colors, the men are paid sixpence a day.
  The troops of the Standing Army, (United Kingdom,) March, 1885, were proportionately distributed as follows: forty-three per cent. in England, two per cent. in Scotland, twenty-five per cent. in Ireland, and thirty-five per cent. abroad, not including India.
  For purposes of administration, instruction, and mobili-

Major-General, Sir F. S. Roberts, V.C., K.C.B.
in
ft o
C/3 H-l
d o M"b & - is! ai 3agO oo enMn CO Ol N T'o E o M i nrl i en$e *G V* eo o i. S3 en? cT t oaw 1O OOMc$CO g 5 o 1-H Mids efg l isCO OO COM CO M t.H iE1 il OCO 0i(S0 V bdO V M V a.3SN c ajCO O d sfaM I EXjo0 MHHSO M 6CO J10 013SM MGTj.COsEin aOO .rf ,- COo "c O J O 4J M1aj 1 oH2CO to enCOHIK O a. t-. . . . .O J.11/. Engla 'rt ' e *S* 5al0I'g'iS I §rt rt 2 H- 11 8. ..
I -,
I!

C. J3

zation, Great Britain and Ireland are partitioned into thirteen military districts commanded by general officers. These are sub-divided as follows: for the infantry one hundred and two sub-districts under regimental commanders ; for the artillery there are twelve sub-districts, and for the cavalry two districts. The brigade of an infantry sub-district comprises usually two line battalions, two militia battalions, the brigade depot, rifle volunteer corps, and infantry of the army reserve. Of the line battalions one is generally at home and one abroad. In an artillery sub-district are comprised a proportion of the royal artillery and artillery of the militia, volunteers, and army reserve respectively. In like manner a cavalry sub-district includes the yeomanry and army reserve cavalry.

The officers on duty in the Adjutant-General's and Quartermaster's departments of the British army are, as a rule, detailed for a term of five years from the Line, but must rejoin their regiments immediately upon orders for foreign service.

The Royal Engineers then were and are organized into forty-three companies.

The cavalry is divided into the Household Cavalry and Cavalry of the Line. The first named comprises the 1st and 2d Life Guards and Royal Horse Guards,|three regiments. The Line is composed of twenty-eight regiments, as follows : seven of dragoon guards, three of dragoons, thirteen of hussars, five of lancers. Thestrength of regiments varies from 450 to 625 men with from 300 to 400 troop horses each.

The artillery|under the title of the Royal Regiment of Artillery|is divided into three classes ; the Royal Horse Artillery of two brigades of twelve batteries each, making a brigade total of sixty guns ; the Field Artillery of four brigades of seventy-six batteries, and the Garrison Artillery of eleven brigades. For the non-professional reader it may be well to say that, in the horse artillery, all the *personnel of* a battery is mounted, the better to act with cavalry or mounted infantry ; under the general term " field artillery" may be classed mountain batteries (only maintained in India), field batteries proper, in which the guns are somewhat heavier, and served by gunners who are not mounted, but on occasion are carried on the limbers and on seats attached to the axles, and in an emergency may be carried on the " off" horses of teams. Under the class "field artillery," also, would come such large guns as are required in war for siege or other heavy operations, and which in India or Afghanistan would be drawn by bullocks.

The infantry is composed of the Guards, the Line, and the Rifles. The Guards consist of three regiments| Grenadier Guards, Coldstream Guards, and Scots Fusilier Guards; in all seven battalions. The Line comprises IO2 regiments (204 battalions); the Rifles four battalions. Besides these there are two regiments of' Colonial (West India) colored troops.

The Militia is intended for local defence, but can be ordered anywhere within the United Kingdom, and is available for garrison duty in the Mediterranean. Enlistment in the militia is for six years. The officers are commissioned by the Queen, and, as before noted, all the details of control and recruitment are entrusted to district commanders. For instruction this force may be called out, for a period not to exceed eight weeks annually, with regular officers as instructors. There are 212 battalions of infantry, 25 brigades of garrison artillery, and 3 regiments of engineers comprised in this force.

The Militia Reserve, limited to one fourth of the active militia, is liable to army service in case of an emergency, and for the term of six years is entitled to $i per annum.

The Volunteers represent " the bulwark " in case of invasion ; they are organized principally as garrison artillery and infantry. The officers are commissioned by the county lieutenants, subject to the approval of the Queen. The men are recruited, armed, and instructed by the Government. Recruits are required to attend thirty drills, and afterward not less than nine drills annually. The volunteer force is composed of 278 battalions of infantry, 46 brigades of garrison artillery and 15 battalions of engineers.

The Yeomanry Cavalry are equipped as light cavalry, drill eight days per year, and are subject to call in case of riot and insurrection, when each man with a horse receives seven pence a day. There are thirty-eight regiments.

The Army of India differs from that of the United Kingdom, not only in its composition, but in the character of its organization. This organization dates from 1858, when the government passed from the East India Company to the Crown.

The European regiments serving in India are in all respects organized and maintained, as in England. In each presidency forming the three political subdivisions, and among which the Anglo-Indian army is distributed, exists a staff corps which supplies all European officers permitted to serve with native troops. These officers must pass certain examinations before they can be assigned to any of the following vacancies in any native regiment.

INDIAN REGIMENT.
EUROPEANS
I Commandant,
I Second-in-command
and wing officer,

   1 Wing-officer,
   2 Wing-subalterns,
I Adjutant,

1 Quartermaster,
1 Medical officer.

2 Subadars (captains), 1st class, 2 " " 2d "
4 " " 3d "
4 Jemandars (lieuts.), 1st "
4 " " zd "

1 Havildar (sergt.-major),
40 Havildars (sergeants),
40 Naicks (corporals),
16 Drummers,
600 Sepoys (privates).

The duties of the commandant of a native regiment correspond in general to those of a similar officer in a European corps. Three times a week he holds a " durbar," for the trial of. offenders and transaction of general regimental business. The men are paid by the native officers in presence of the European " Wing-officer," whois responsible for all public property issued to his half battalion, or wing.

The native officers are commissioned by the Indian Government, and, as a rule, are promoted from the ranks, and are of the same caste as the privates. Certain native officers of the engineers and artillery may be eligible to appointment in the corresponding European corps ; one is always assigned as an aide-de-camp to the Viceroy. When on detailed service, a native officer is allowed to command his company, but " no battalion parades should take place without the presence of a British officer." In each regiment there is a drill-sergeant and drill-corporal, who receive extra pay for their services. Corporals are promoted from privates who know how to read and write in at least one character, or who have displayed extraordinary courage. The pay per month of a sepoy is equal to $3.50; havildar, $7; jemandar, $17.50 ; subadar, $33.50 to $50. European officers with native regiments: commandant, $620; wing-officers, $302 to $322; adjutant, $237.86; quartermaster, $187.86; medical officers, $300, monthly. The annual pay-roll of a native regiment of 720 combatants and 45 non-combatants amounts to about $69,114. In consideration of the pay each sepoy is required to provide his rations and clothing, except one coat and one pair of trousers issued by the Government every two years; in consequence, each regiment is accompanied by a native village called a bazaar, containing tradesmen of all kinds; this bazaar is under strict discipline and is managed by the quartermaster. The entire outfit follows the regiment into the field.

Indian Army Regulations.

Colonel Gordon of the Indian army testifies : " With regard to native troops under a cannonade I may say that I saw our native infantry twice under the fire of the Afghan mountain guns, and they behaved very steadily and coolly. Ammunition was economically expended. I attributed much the small loss sustained by the troops in Afghanistan to our excellent straight shooting."

The cavalry of India has in certain instances borne an excellent reputation for efficiency in action, is well set up, and in its instruction and discipline is modelled after the British system. The artillery comprises well-instructed native organizations, but its principal experience has been with light field guns against irregular troops. The Achilles heel of the Indian army consists in this, that there are but eight European officers to each regiment, and of these but six would be available to lead in battle : the quartermaster and surgeon being at such a time otherwise engaged. The native officers, seldom having an opportunity to command in Peace, would be unreliable leaders in such an emergency. At the action of Ali Musjid, November 21, 1878, the day before the occupation of that fort, six British officers of a native battalion were placed *hors de combat,* so that on the first day after crossing the Afghan frontier there was but one European officer to manage the regiment.

Besides the regular establishment there are about *10,000* European volunteers (including 4,000 railway officials and employes) available for local defence.

The feudatory chiefs of India enjoy an aggregate revenue of some .$15,000,000, equal to more than one third of the income of the British Government of India. They maintain forces aggregating 350,000 men with 4,000 guns to perform the duties of court ceremonial, garrison, military police, guards, and escorts, throughout territories aggregating nearly 600,000 square miles with 50,000,000 of inhabitants. These forces are unreservedly held at the disposal of the Crown by the native Princes.

Transport and Supply.|This essential feature of all wars will be briefly considered in the light of the Anglo- Afghan War of 1879-80. Large quantities of supplies were transported from the main base of operations on the Indus, and distributed to the troops in the field over four or five distinct lines of communication, and over roads and mountain paths of varied degrees of ruggedness. The country on both sides of the Indo-Afghan frontier was severely taxed to furnish the necessary animals. Part of the transport was hired|and as in the case of the Brahuis camels|with the services of the owners, who were easily offended and likely to decamp with their property in a night. During the first year the system was under the direct control of the commissariat department ; but as this proved unsatisfactory, in the subsequent campaign it was entirely reorganized and superintended by an officer of engineers, with a large number of officers from the Line to assist. This gave better satisfaction. Immense numbers of camels died from heat, overwork, irregular food, and neglect. Owing to the dryness of the climate and intense heat of the summer the bullock-carts were perpetually falling to pieces. The mules, donkeys, and ponies gave the best results, but do not abound in sufficient quantities to enable an army in Afghanistan to dispense with camels. A successful experiment in rafting, from Jelalabad to Dakka, was tried. The rafts consisted of inflated skins lashed together with a light framework; between June 4-13, seven thousand skins were used, and, in all, 885 soldiers and one thousand tons of stores were transported forty miles down the Kabul River, the journey taking five hours. A great deal of road-making and repairing was done under the supervision of the transport corps. A system of " stages " or relays of pack-animals or carts was organized, by which a regular quantity of supplies was forwarded over the main lines, daily, with almost the regularity, if not the speed, of rail carriage. The great number of animals employed required a corresponding force of attendants, inspectors, and native doctors, all of whom served to make up that excessive army of " followers" for which Anglo-Indian expeditions are famous. Drivers were

Of a train of eighteen hundred unloaded camels on the road from Dadur to Jacobabad, for six days in June, six hundred died of exhaustion. In March, 1855 Col. Green, C.B., lost one hundred and seventeen horses out of four hundred, from the heat, during a march of thirty miles.

required at the following rate : one driver for each pair of bullocks, every four camels, every three mules and ponies, every six donkeys.

The great obstacle to the satisfactory operation of the transport system was its novelty and experimental character, and that its organization had to be combined with its execution. Besides which, cholera broke out in June and swept away three hundred employes. Grazing camps were established in the neighborhood of the Bolan Pass for the bullocks, and aqueducts built for the conveyance of a water supply ; one of these was of masonry, more than a mile in length, from Dozan down to the Bolan. It has been stated that grazing was scarce in the region of the Bolan: in 1879 more than four thousand bullocks were grazed there during the summer, and large quantities of forage were cut for winter use.

Any prolonged military operations in Afghanistan must, to a certain extent, utilize hired transport, although there are many objections urged.

Sir Richard Temple said (1879): " That the amount of transport required for active service, such as the late campaign in Afghanistan, is so great that to hire transport is synonymous to pressing it from the people of the district from which it is hired, and impressment of the means of transport must lead to impressment of drivers, whonaturally (having no interest whatever in the campaign in which they are called upon to serve) render the most unwilling service and take the earliest opportunity of rendering their animals unserviceable in hopes of escaping a distasteful duty. This service is frequently so unpopular that, sooner than leave the boundaries of their native country, the impressed drivers desert, leaving their animals in the hands of the transport authorities or take them away with them. For the above reasons I should recommend that all transport for a campaign should be the property of Government."

The average carrying power of certain kinds of transport, in pounds, is as follows : *bullock-carts* (with two pairs), on fairly level ground, 1,400 ; on hilly ground, 1,000 ; (with one pair) on fairly level ground, 850 ; on hilly ground, 650 ; *camels,* 400; *mules,* 200 ; *ponies,* 175 ; *men,* 50.

In commenting on this subject, Lord Wolseley relates that when serving in China with Indian troops he " awoke one morning and found that all our drivers had bolted. Our transport consisted of carts supplied by the Chinese Government, by contractors, and by the country generally. I do not think that the carts had been carried away, but all the mules and men had disappeared except three drivers who belonged to me. I was very much astonished that these men had not bolted also. I had a small detachment of cavalry with me and a very excellent duffadar in charge of it. I asked him how he had managed to keep these drivers|having some time before said that unless he looked after them well he would never get to Pekin. He replied, with some hesitation: ' I remember what you told me, and the fact is I tied the tails of those three men together, overnight, and then tied them to the tent pole, and put a man over them.'"

The Elephant, like the stage coach, finds his field of usefulness, as a means of transport, growing smaller by degrees. He is still a feature in India, and has been used for military purposes to some extent in the eastern part of Afghanistan. He will doubtless form part of the means of transportation employed by the British forces near their present base, and in rear of the Kabul-Kandahar line, and for that reason is noticed here.

The Superintendent of the Government Elephant Khed- dahs at Dakka has given us, in a recent paper, much information concerning the elephant in freedom and captivity. He does not claim a high order of intelligence, but rather of extraordinary obedience and docility for this animal. Very large elephants are exceptional. Twice round the forefoot gives the height at the shoulder ; few females attain the height of eight feet; " tuskers," or male elephants, vary from eight to nine feet; the Maharajah of Nahur, Sirmoor, possesses one standing ten feet five and one half inches. The age varies from 80 to 150 years, according to the best authorities, and it is recorded that those familiar with the haunts of the wild elephant have never found the bones of an elephant that had died a natural death. In freedom they roam in herds of thirty to fifty, always led by a female; mature about twenty-

The use of elephants in transporting field guns in Afghanistan is emphatically discouraged by those who served with it last; very few flankers were employed to protect the Elephant artillery used in the Kuram valley, and its success can only be interpreted by supposing the direct interposition of Providence or the grossest stupidity to our feeble enemy.

Elephant with Artillery ; on the Road to Al i Musjid.

five. In India the males only have tusks ; in Ceylon only the females. They are fond of the water, swim well, but can neither trot nor gallop ; their only pace is a walk, which may be increased to a *shuffle* of fifteen miles an hour for a very short distance; they cannot leap, and a ditch eight by eight feet would be impassable.

In Bengal and Southern India elephants particularly abound, and seem to be increasing in numbers. In the Billigurungan Hills, a range of three hundred square miles on the borders of Mysore, they made their appearance about eighty years ago ; yet prior to that time this region was under high cultivation, traces of orchards, orange groves, and iron-smelting furnaces remaining in what is now a howling wilderness. Elephants are caught in stockades or kraals. The Government employs hunting parties of 350 natives trained to the work, and more than 100 animals are sometimes secured in a single drive.

New elephants are trained by first rubbing them down with bamboo rods, and shouting at them, and by tying them with ropes; they are taught to kneel by taking them into streams about five feet deep, when the sun is hot, and prodding them on the back with sharp sticks.

The total number of elephants maintained is eight hundred, of which one half are used for military purposes. They consume about 400 pounds of green, or 250 pounds of dry fodder daily, and are also given unhusked rice.An elephant is expected to carry about 1,200 pounds with ease. In the Abyssinian Expedition elephants travelled many hundreds of miles, carrying from 1,500 to 1,800 pounds (including their gear), but out of forty-four, five died from exhaustion ; they are capable of working from morning to night, or of remaining under their loads for twenty hours at a stretch.

Elephants have been known to swim a river three hundred yards wide with the hind legs tied together.

An elephant's gear consists of *gaddcla,* or quilted cloth, i.j. inches thick, reaching half-way down his sides and from the neck to the croup. On this is placed the *guddu,* or pad, 6x5 feet and 9 inches thick, formed of stout sacking stuffed with dried grass. The whole is girthed with a long rope passed twice around the body, round the neck as a breast-strap, and under the tail as a crupper. The whole weighs 200 pounds. An improvement upon this has been made by our authority (Mr. Sanderson), which seems to bear the same relation to the old gear that the open McClellan saddle does to the ordinary British hunting saddle. It consists (see illustration) of two pads entirely detached, each 4 feet long, 15 inches wide, and 6 inches thick, made of blanket covered with tarpaulin, and encased in stout sacking. One is placed on each side of the elephant's spine, and retained there by two iron arches. There is no saddle-cloth, the load rests on the ribs; the breaststrap and crupper hook into rings on the saddle; there are rings to fasten the load to; it weighs 140 pounds. With foot-boards it is convenient for riding; a cradle can also be attached for carrying field guns. Recent experiments have shown the practicability of conveying elephants by rail in ordinary open cattle-trucks; they were indifferent to the motion, noises, or bridges ; it is said that 32 elephants could be thus carried on one train.

There is no "elephant gun-drill" laid down in the Imperial Regulations, but when the gun goes into action the elephant is made to kneel, and long "skids " are placed against the cradle upon which the gun rests, so as to form an inclined plane to the ground. The gun is then lifted off the cradle and down the skids by levers and tackle.

The excellent railway facilities for moving troops and supplies to the Indo-Afghan frontier were described in 1880, by Traffic Manager Ross, of the Scinde, Punjab, and Delhi Railway, before the United Service Institution of India.

He stated that experiments had been made by the military and railway authorities in loading and disembarking troops and war *materiel,* and that much experience had been afforded by the Afghan operations of 1878-9.

The movement of troops to and from the frontier commenced in October, 1878, and ended June, 1879. During that period were conveyed over his road 190,0x30 men, 33,000 animals, 500 guns, 112,000,000 pounds of military stores. The maximum number carried in any one month was in November|40,000 men, 8,000 animals, and 20,800, ooo pounds of stores. The greatest number of special trains run in one day was eight, carrying 4,100 men, 300 animals, and 800,000 pounds of stores. As an instance of rapid loading, when the loth Bengal Cavalry left for Malta, 80 horses were loaded on a train in 10 minutes*JScale /4-inch ='!-foot*

from the ordinary station platform ; the pack-ponies gave more trouble, having in some cases to be picked up bodily and pushed into the car. The average time taken in loading up a squadron of cavalry, comprising 8 officers, 128 men, 92 followers, 150 horses, and 10,800 pounds of baggage and ammunition, was from i hour to 90 minutes. Great difficulty was found in loading camels, for which a sling and crane is required. The speed of troop-trains was about 21 miles an hour. No accidents occurred. Mr.

Ross stated that in case of emergency, 11 trains each way could be run over the Lahore and Mooltan section, and 15 trains each way over the Lahore and Delhi section ; this was the maximum number of trains capable of 20 miles an hour with 35 cars, allowing for crossings and other necessary halts. At this rate 3 batteries of artillery, 2 regiments of cavalry, and 5 regiments of infantry (7,000 men), could be concentrated at Lahore every 24 hours. And by this line alone, 70,000 men, with guns, horses, and stores complete, could be brought to Lahore in 10 days. As the native troops prefer cars without seats, ordinary box-cars are always ready; 30 to 35 natives, or 8 horses, can be carried in a car. This is the railway leading to Kurrachee, the seaport nearest to Quetta. Experience has shown that there is but little trouble to .accumulate large stores of provisions for an army, particularly in or near the Indo-Afghan frontier, provided there is a force to distribute it. Compressed food and forage "were not used in 1878, but it may be supposed that they will form part of the present British supplies. Medicine was often deficient and illiberally issued.

Intelligence.|During the later campaigns in Afghanistan, the British Commanding General has been invested with supreme political authority, and the Political Department (which is a branch of the Foreign Department of the Government of India) has been under his control; a political officer was generally assigned to the staff of each independent army commander, and has had charge of all military intelligence; these officers were familiar with the language and habits of the Afghans, and were also useful in obtaining supplies from the natives. The information, obtained daily, in this way and through the ordinary military scouts, was sifted and compiled in the Quartermaster-General's office for the information of the Commanding General. Maps of the country were supplied to all officers. The Heliograph was used with marked success in signalling in that mountainous country. Messages were sent from Kabul to Jamrud, 190 miles, with but four. intermediate stations, and again between Kabul and Gun-damuck, seventy-five miles, with but one station. Our information as to the status of the Political Officer is based upon a. report made by Col. Chapman, R. A., but is supplemented by the views of Lieut. Martin, R. E., who, served with the same column. He says:

" The old English respect for law and constituted civif authority is often carried to extravagance, and notably in India, where the Roman maxim 'Inter armes silent leges'"appears to have been clean forgotten. The Politicals were by no means silent, and the amount of knowledge they possessed of border statistics was something marvellous. Did any step appear to the military sense advisable, there was a much better, though less comprehensible, *political* reason why it should not be undertaken. The oracle has spoken and the behest must be obeyed. An enemy in sight who became afterwards hostile, must not be kept at a distance; through political glasses they appear as ' children of nature,' while the country out of sight must not be explored, the susceptibilities of the sensitive ' Tammizais' having to be respected. That much valuable service was performed by political officers there can be no doubt, but that they caused great exasperation among soldiers cannot be denied, and the example of the War of 1839-40 causes them to be looked upon as a very possible source of danger."

Anglo-Afghan Operations. |The observations of a participant in the last British campaign in Afghanistan will be found of value in the study of future operations in that country. Of the Afghan tactics he says: " The enemy (generally speaking, a race of Highlanders) vastly preferred the attack, and usually obtained the advantage of superior numbers before risking an attack; being able to dispense (for the time) with lines of communication and baggage and commissariat columns, the Afghan tribes were often able to raise large gatherings on chosenground. They could always attack us; we were rarely able (except when they chose) to find them at home." This observer says the regular troops of the Ameer were not so formidable as the tribal gatherings. The presence of a tactically immovable artillery hinders the action of an Asiatic army. The mounted men are usually the first to leave when the fight is going against their side in a general engagement. One of the best specimens of their tactics was at Ahmed-Kheyl, on the Ghazni-Kandahar road, when the British division was one hundred miles from any support. The Afghans assembled a force outnumbering the British ten to one. The attack was made in a series of rushes, twice dispersing the British cavalry, and once driving back the infantry. Exposed to a constant fire of field guns, the Afghans stood their ground, although poorly armed with a variety of obsolete weapons |from an Enfield to a handjar or a stick. Trouble may always be expected from the night attacks of certain tribes like the Alizais and Waziris.

Lieut. Martin, R. E. *(Journal U. S. I. of India).*

The English infantry formation was an objectionably close one, and Lieut. Martin says that the bayonets and rifle-barrels of the front rank were sometimes struck and jammed *by bullets from the rear rank.* The action of the English cavalry, as at Ahmed-Kheyl, was suicidal in receiving the enemy's charge|practically at a halt. Occasionally shelter trenches were used, but disapproved.

In the Kuram valley column, under General Roberts, the cavalry (principally native, with one regular squadronand a battery of horse artillery) formed a brigade, but was never used independently, nor was it instructed (although well equipped) for modern cavalry work. The opposition to dismounted cavalry duty is still so great, in the British army, that the mounted arm is paralyzed for effective service.

Very little was done by the horse artillery with the Kuram column. In the case of the field artillery it was found necessary on two occasions to transfer the ammunition boxes from the bullock-carts to the backs of elephants, on account of the steepness of the hills. The mountain artillery (native) was the most serviceable ; a Catling battery, packed on ponies, and in charge of a detachment of Highlanders, was never used however.

The armament of the infantry included both Martini and Snider rifles, requiring two kinds of ammunition, but, as the service by pack-mules was ample, no confusion ensued, although Lieut. Martin says: " In one case I heard a whisper that a regimental reserve of ammunition was found to be *blank cartridges,* but this must be a heavy joke." Intrenching tools were carried on camels. A mixture of military and civil-engineer administration and operation is mentioned as unsatisfactory in results. There was great difficulty in getting tools and materials at' the opening of the campaign|particularly those required for road and bridge work, although a railroad within two hundred miles had a large stock on hand.

The art of camping and rough fortification was well practised. The best defended camp was surrounded by bush abatis and flanked by half-moon *sungas* of boulder- stone work, which held the sentries. The most approved permanent camps or " posts " were mud *serais* flanked by bastions at the alternate angles and overlooking a yard or " kraal." These were established about ten miles apart, to protect communications, and furnished frequent patrols. During the latter part of the campaign these outposts were manned by the native contingents of the Punjab who volunteered.

The rapid march of General Roberts from Kabul to Kandahar in August, 1880, and the final dispersion of the forces of Ayoub Khan, illustrated British operations in Afghanistan under the most favorable circumstances. The forces included 2,800 European and 7,000 Indian troops ; no wheeled artillery was taken ; one regiment of native infantry, trained to practical engineering work, did the work of sappers and miners ; for the transportation of sick and wounded 2,000 doolie-bearers, 286 ponies, and 43 donkeys; for transport of supplies a pack-train of 1,589 yabus, 4,510 mules, 1,224 Indian ponies, 912 donkeys|a total of 10,148 troops, 8,143 native followers, and 11,224 animals, including cavalry horses; 30 days' rations, of certain things, and dependence on the country for fresh meat and forage. The absence of timber on this route rendered it difficult to obtain fuel except by burning the roofs of the villages and digging up the roots of " Southern-wood " for this purpose. The manner of covering the movement

t-r U

rested with the cavalry commander. Usually the front was covered by two regiments, one regiment on each flank, at a mile from the column, detaching one or more troops as rear-guard; once movement had commenced, the animals, moving at different gaits were checked as little as possible. With such a number of non-combatants the column was strung out for six or seven miles, and the rear-guard leaving one camp at 7 A.M. rarely reached the next|fifteen to twenty miles distant|before sundown.

Routes.|For operations in Afghanistan the general British base is the frontier from Kurrachee to Peshawur. These points are connected by a railway running east of the Indus, which forms a natural boundary to the Indian frontier, supplemented by a line of posts which are from north to south as follows: Jumrud, Baru, Mackeson, Michni, Snub Kadar, Abazai, and Kohut; also by fortified posts connected by military roads,|Thull, Bunnoo, and Doaba.

From the Indus valley into the interior of Afghanistan there are only four lines of communication which can be called military roads: first, from *Peshawur* through the Khaiber Pass to *Kabul;* second, from *Thull,* over the Peiwar and Shuturgurdan passes to *Kabul;* third, from *Dera Ismail Khan* through the Guleir Surwandi and Sargo passes to *Ghazni;* fourth, by *Quetta* to Kandahar and thence to *Herat,* or by Ghazni to *Kabul.* Besides these there are many steep, difficult, mule tracks over the bleak, barren, Sulimani range, which on its eastern side*s*

"s cis very precipitous and impassable for any large body of troops.

The Peshawur-Kabul road, 170 miles long, was in 1880 improved and put in good order. From Peshawur the road gradually rises, and after 7 miles reaches Jumrud (1,650 feet elevation), and 44 miles further west passes through the great Khaiber

Pass. This pass, 31 miles long, can, however, be turned by going to the north through the Absuna and Tartara passes ; they are not practicable for wheels, and the first part of the road along the Kabul River is very difficult and narrow, being closed in by precipitous cliffs.

As (ar as Fort Ali Musjid the Khaiber is a narrow defile between perpendicular slate rocks 1,460 feet high ; beyond that fort the road becomes still more difficult, and in some of the narrowest parts, along the rocky beds of torrents, it is not more than 56 feet wide. Five miles further it passes through the valley of Lalabeg 1 miles wide by 6 miles long, and then after rising for four miles it reaches the top of the Pass, which from both sides offers very strong strategical positions. From thence it descends for 2$ miles to the village of Landi Khana (2,463 feet), which lies in a gorge about a quarter of a mile wide ; then on to Dakka (altitude 1,979 feet). This pass, loo to 225 feet wide and 60 feet long, is shut in by steep but not high slopes, overgrown with bushes.

On the eleven miles'march from Dakka to Hazarnao, the Khurd Khaiber is passed, a deep ravine about one mile

long, and in many places so narrow that tv/o horsemen cannot pass each other. Hazarnao is well cultivated, and rich in fodder; 15 miles farther is Chardeh (1,800 feet altitude), from which the road passes through a well-cultivated country, and on through the desert of Surkh Den- kor (1,892 feet altitude), which is over 8J miles from Jela- labad. From this city (elsewhere described) onward as far as Gundamuck the route presents no great difficulties; it passes through orchards, vineyards, and cornfields to the Surkhab River; but beyond this three spurs of the Safed Koh range, running in a northeastern direction, have to be surmounted.

Between Jelalabad and Kabul two roads can be followed: the first crosses the range over the Karkacha Pass (7,925 feet alt.) at the right of which is Assin Kilo, thence through the Kotul defile, and ascending the Khurd Kabul f (7,397 feet alt.) to the north reaches the high plateau on which Kabul is situated; the other leads over the short but dangerous Jagdallak Pass to Jagdallak, from which there are three roads to Kabull the northernmost over the Khinar and the third over the Sokhta passes; all these, more difficult than the Khaiber, are impassable during the winter. It was here, as already related, that the greater part of Elphinstone's command, in 1842, perished. There is a dearth of fuel and supplies

The heat at Jelalabad from the end of April is tremendousl105 to IIO in the shade.

The Khurd Kabul Pass is about five miles long, with an impetuous mountain torrent which the road (1842) crossed twenty-eight times.

by this line of communication. The second, or Thull- Kuram-Kabul, route, was taken by General Roberts in 1878-9. It extends from Thull, one of the frontier posts already mentioned, some forty miles into the Kuram valley, and then inclining towards the west leads to the Kuram fort (Mohammed Azim's), a walled quadrangular fortress with flanking towers at an elevation of 6,000 feet. The Kuram valley is, up to this point, well cultivated and productive ; wood, water, and forage abound. Winter only lasts with any severity for six weeks, and the Spring and Autumn are delightful.

A short distance above the fort commences the ascent toward the Peiwar Pass (8,000 feet alt.), twenty-four miles distant. The road, thickly bordered with cedar and pine trees, is covered with boulders and is very difficult, and from the village of Peiwarlone of many *en route,* of the usual Afghan fortified typelit leads through a winding defile to the top of the pass. Here the road is confined by perpendicular chalk rocks, the summits of which are covered with scrub timber and a luxuriant growth of laurel. On the farther side of the pass the road ascends to the height of the Hazardarakht, (which is covered with snow in the winter), and then climbs to the Shuturgurdan Pass (1 1,375 feet alt.), reaching a plateau on which the snow lies for six months of the year; thence it descends into the fertile Logar valley and reaches Akton Khel, which is only fifty-one miles from Kabul. The total length of this route is about 175 miles.

The third, or Dera-Ismail-Khan-Sargo-Ghazni, route passes through a region less frequented than those mentioned, and is not thought sufficiently difficult for detailed description. Passing due west, through seventy miles of mountain gorges destitute of supplies or forage, it debouches, through the Gomal Pass, into a more promising country, in which forage may be obtained. At this point it branches to Ghazni, Kandahar, and Pishin respectively. A road exists from Mooltan, crossing the Indus at Dera-Ghazi-Khan, Mithunkot, Rajanpur, Rojan, Lalgoshi, Dadur to Quetta, and was utilized by General Biddulph, from whose account of his march from the Indus to the Helmund, in 1879, ls gleaned the following. The main point of concentration for the British forces, either from India or from England via Kurrachee is thus minutely described.

" The western frontier of India is, for a length of *600* miles, bounded by Biluchistan and territories inhabited by Biluch tribes, and for 300 miles Biluch country intervenes between our border and Afghanistan. The plains of the Punjab and Sind run along the boundary of Biluchistan, and at a distance of from 25 to 50 miles the Indus pursues a course, as far down as Mithunkot, from north to south, and then winds south-west through a country similar to that of Egypt. A belt of cultivation and beyond that the desert this line of hills (the Eastern Sulimani) extends as a continuous rampart with the plains running up to the foot of the range, and havingan elevation of 11,000 feet at the Tukl-i-Suliman, and of 7,40x3 near Fort Munro (opposite Dera-Ghazi-Khan), gradually diminishes in height and dwindles away till it is lost in the plains near Kusmore, at a point 12 miles from the Indus. The strip of low-land country on the west bank of the Indus up to the foot of the hills is called the *Derajat.* It is cut up and broken by torrents, the beds of which are generally dry wastes, and the country is, except at a few places where permanent water is found, altogether sterile and hot. If we view the physical aspect looking north and north-west from Jacobabad, we notice a wide bay of plains extending between the broken spur of the Sulimani, and a second range of hills having a direction parallel to the outer range. This plain is called the Kachi, extends in an even surface for 150 miles from the Indus at Sukkur, and is bounded on the north by successive spurs lying between the two great ranges. The Kachi, thus bounded by barren hills on all sides but the south, is one of the hottest regions in the world. Except where subject to inundations or within reach of irrigation it is completely sterilela hard clay surface called *Pat,*| and this kind of country extends around to the east of the spur of thc Suliman into the Derajat country. Subject to terrific heats and to a fiercely hot pestilential wind, the Kachi is at times fatal even to the natives."

The range of mountains bounding the Kachi to the westward is a continuous wall with imperceptible breaks only, and it bears the local names of Gindari, Takari, and Entrance to the Polan Pass, from Dadur.

Kirthar. Through this uniform rampart there are two notable rents or defiles, viz.: the *Mulla* opening opposite Gundana, leading to Kelat; and the *Bolan* entering near Dadur, leading to Quetta, Kandahar, and Herat. The Bolan is an abrupt defilela rent in the range,|the bottom filled with the pebbly bed of a mountain torrent. This steep ramp forms for sixty miles the road from Dadur, elevation 750 feet, to the Dasht-i-Bedowlat, elevation 6,225 feet. This inhospitable plateau and the upper portion of the Bolan are subject to the most piercingly cold winds and temperature; and the sudden change from the heat of the Kachi to the cold above is most trying to the strongest constitutions. Notwithstanding the difficulties of the road, the absence of supplies and fuel, and the hostile character of the predatory tribes around, this route has been always most in favor as the great commercial and military communication from Persia, Central Asia, and Khorassan to India.

The causes which led to the establishment of a British garrison at Quetta are not unlike those which are urged as good Russian reasons for the occupation of territory in certain parts of Central Asia. Briefly stated, it seems that after the conquest of the Punjab, the proximity of certain disturbed portions of Biluchistan, and the annoyance suffered by various British military expeditions, in 1839-1874, from certain tribes of Biluchis|notably the Maris and Bugtis,|made it desirable that more decisive measures should be adopted. In 1876 a force of Britishtroops was marched to Kelat, and by mutual agreement .with the Khan a political agency was established at Quetta, ostensibly to protect an important commercial highway, but at the same time securing a military footing of great value. But the character of the lords of the soil |the Maris, for instance|has not changed for the better, and the temporary general European occupation of the country would afford an opportunity to gratify their predatory instincts, which these bandits would not hesitate to utilize. The Maris can put 2,000 men into the field and march 100 miles to make an attack. When they wish to start upon a raid they collect their wise men together and tell the warriors where the cattle and the corn are. If the reports of spies, sent forward, confirm this statement, the march is undertaken. They ride upon mares which make no noise ; they travel only at night. They are the most excellent outpost troops in the world. When they arrive at the scene of action a perfect watch is kept and information by single messengers is secretly sent back. Every thing being ready a rush of horsemen takes place, the villages are surrounded, the cattle swept away, the women and children hardly used|fortunate if they escape with their lives. The villagars have their fortlets to retreat to, and, if they reach them, can pull the ladders over after them and fire away from their towers. Dadur is an insignificant town at the foot of the Bolan. From here the Kandahar road leads for sixty miles through the Pass|a gradual ascent; in winter there isnot a mouthful of food in the entire length of the defile.

Quetta, compared with the region to the south, appears a very Garden of Eden. It is a small oasis, green and well watered.

From Quetta to Pishin the road skirts the southern border of a vast plain, interspersed with valleys, which extend across the eastern portion of Afghanistan toward the

Russian dominion. A study of the Pishin country shows that it is, on its northwestern side supported on a limb of the Western Sulimani. This spur, which defines the west of the Barshor valley, is spread out into the broad plateau of Toba, and is then produced as a continuous ridge, dividing Pishin from the plains of Kadani, under the name of Khoja Amran. The Barshor is a deep bay of the plain, and there is an open valley within the outer screen of hills. A road strikes off here to the Ghilzai country and to Ghazni. Though intersected by some very low and unimportant hills and ridges, the Pishin plains and those of Shallkot may be looked upon as one feature. We may imagine the Shall Valley the vestibule, the Kujlak-Kakur Vale the passage, the Gayud Yara Plain an antechamber, and Pishin proper the great *salle*. Surrounded by mountains which give forth an abundant supply of water, the lands bordering on the hills are studded with villages, and there is much cultivation; there is a total absence of timber, and the cultivation of fruit-trees has been neglected. The Lora rivers cutting into the plain interferes somewhat with the construction of roads.

The Plain of Pishin possesses exceptional advantages for the concentration and rendezvous of large bodies of troops, and has already been utilized for that purpose by the British.

From the Khoja Amran, looking toward Kandahar, the plains, several thousand feet below, are laid out like a sea, and the mountains run out into isolated promontories ; to the left the desert is seen like a turbulent tide about to overflow the plains.

The rivers on the Quetta-Kandahar route do not present much impediment to the passage of troops in dry weather, but in flood they become serious obstacles and cannot be.passed until the waters retire.

The ascent from the east through the Khojak Pass is easy, the descent on the west very precipitous. A thirteen-foot cart road was made, over the entire length of twenty miles, by General Biddulph in 1878-9, by which the first wheeled vehicles, which ever reached Khorassan from India, passed.

From Kandahar (elsewhere described)|which is considered by General Hamley and other authorities, one of the most important strategic points in any scheme of permanent defence for India|diverge two main roads: one a continuation of the Quetta-Herat route bearing N. W., and one running N. E. to Kabul.

Gen. Biddulph says: "The position of Kandahar near to the slopes of the range to the westward of the city renders it impossible to construct works close at handto cover the road from Herat. The high ridge and outlying hills dividig Kandahar and its suburbs from the Argandab valley completely command all the level ground between the city and the pass. Beyond the gap a group of detached mountains extends, overlooking the approaches, and follows the left bank of the Argandab as far down as Panjwai, fifteen miles distant. Positions for defensive works must be sought, therefore, in front of that place on the right bank of the river. To the N. E. of Kandahar the open plain affords situations for forts, well removed from the hills, at a short distance, and at Akhund Ziarut, thirty miles on the road to Ghazni, there is a gorge which would, if held, add to security on that quarter."

The country between Kandahar and the Helmund has the same general characteristics|plains and mountain spurs alternately,|and while generally fit for grazing is, except in a few spots, unfit for cultivation.

According to the eminent authority just quoted, the great natural strategic feature of this route is the elevated position of Atta Karez, thirty-one miles from Kandahar. He says: "On the whole road this is the narrowest gateway, and this remarkable feature and the concentration of roads here, give to Atta Karez a strategic importance unequalled by any other spot between India and Central Asia."

The roads which meet at Atta.Karez are: the great Herat highway passing through Kokeran and crossing the Argandab opposite Sinjari, whence it lies along the open plain all the way to Atta Karez ; the road which crosses the Argandab at Panjwai; and the road from Taktipul towards Herat.

General Biddulph examined this position carefully in 1879, and discovered a site for a work which would command the valley of the Argandab and sweep the elevated open plain toward the west and northwest.

Abbaza is a village at the crossing of the Herat road over the Helmund, forty-six miles west of Atta Karez. On the west bank lies the ancient castle of Girishk. The country between the Argandab and the Helmund is rolling and inclining gradually from the hills toward the junction of these rivers. The plateau opposite Girishk is 175 feet above the river, which it commands.

The Helmund has already been described. There are numerous fords, but, at certain times, bridges would be required for military purposes. The land in the vicinity of the Helmund is very fertile and seamed with irrigating canals.

From Girishk a road *via* Washir runs through the hills to Herat; this is said to be cool, well supplied with water and grazing, and is a favorite military route. A road, parallel, to the south, goes through Farrah, beyond which both roads blend into one main road to the " Key." Still another road, by Bost, Rudbar, and Lash, along the course of the river, exists. Although not so direct, it is an important route to Herat; upon this road stand the ruins of the ancient city of Bost in a wonderful state of preservation; here, as elsewhere in this region, the remains of fortifications testify to the former military importance of the spot. The citadel of Bost is built on the debris of extensive works and rises 150 feet above the river.

British Generals.|Perhaps the most prominent of modern British commanders, next to Lord Wolseley|is the young and successful soldier, Lieutenant-General Sir Frederick Roberts, G. C. B., C. I. E., commanding the Anglo-Indian Army of the Madras Presidency. He has already seen service in Afghanistan and elsewhere, and has been appointed to the command of one of the principal divisions of the British forces intended to oppose the threatened advance of the Russians on Herat. It was said of him by one of the most brilliant military leaders of the age,| Skobeleff: " For General Roberts I have a great admiration. He seems to me to possess all the qualities of a great general. That was a splendid march of his from Kabul to Kandahar. I think more highly of him than I do of Sir Garnet Wolseley, but there is this to be said of *all your* generals, they have only fought against Asiatic and savage foes. They have not commanded an army against a European enemy, and we cannot tell, therefore, what they are really made of."

The Commander-in-chief of the Army of India, General Sir Donald M. Stewart, G. C. B., C. I. E., to whom has been intrusted the conduct of the British forces in Afghanistan, is also a very distinguished and experienced officer|probably more familiar with the nature of theprobable field of operations than any other in Her Majesty's Service.

Like the United States, the great latent power of England is indisputable, and so long as superiority at sea is maintained, time is given to render that latent power active. For the first year of the coming struggle England must lean heavily upon her navy. Nearly all the regiments of infantry are below the average peace limit, and if filled up simultaneously to a maximum war strength will include more than fifty per cent. of imperfectly trained men, and as the practice has been to fill up those corps ordered abroad with men transferred from other small regiments, it may come to pass that so-called " regular" regiments will consist largely of raw material. Colonel Trench of the British Army says "the organization of the regular cavalry is very defective," and especially complains of the maladministration we have just noted. Demands for cavalry for the Soudan were met by a heavy drain on the already depleted strength of regiments in England'. The Fifth Dragoon Guards, which stood next on the roster for foreign service, gave away nearly two hundred horses and one hundred men. Colonel Trench says that the reserve cavalry have no training, and that there is no reserve of horses. It is doubtful if more than seventy per cent. of the enlisted strength and fifty per cent. of the horses, on paper, could be put in the field now.

Allusion has already been made to the notorious weakness of the British transport system. If this has been the case in the numerous small wars in which her forces have been engaged for the last twentj-five years, what may be expected from the strain of a great international campaign.

On the other hand, Great Britain can boast of an inexhaustible capital, not alone of the revenues which have been accumulating during the last quarter of a century, but of patriotism, physical strength, courage, and endurance, peculiar to a race of conquerors.

Captain Gaisford, who commanded the Khaiber Levies in the Afghan campaign, recommended reforms in the system of transport and supply. He advocated certain American methods, as wind and water-mills to crush and cleanse the petrified and gravelled barley, often issued, and to cut up the inferior hay ; the selection of transport employes who understand animals ; and more care in transporting horses by sea.

5

SECTION 5

IV.
THE RUSSIAN FORCES AND APPROACHES.

A MERE glance at the ponderous military machine with which Russia enforces law and order within her vast domain, and by which she preserves and extends her power, is all that we can give here.

No army in the world has probably undergone, within the last thirty years, such a succession of extensive alterations in organization, in administrative arrangements, and in tactical regulations, as that of Russia. The Crimean War surprised it during a period of transition. Further changes of importance were carried out after that war. Once more, in 1874, the whole military system was remodelled, while ever since the Peace of San Stefano, radical reforms have been in progress, and have been prosecuted with such feverish haste, that it is difficult for the observer to keep pace with them.

The military system of Russia is based upon the principles of universal liability to serve and of territorial distribution. This applies to the entire male population, with certain exemptions or modifications on the ground, respectively, of age or education. Annually there is a " lot- drawing," in which all over twenty, who have not already-drawn lots, must take part. Those who draw blanks are excused from service with the colors, but go into the last reserve, or " Opoltschenie."

Sir L. Graham *(Journal Royal U. S. Institution).* 104

The ordinary term of service is fifteen years,|six with the colors and nine with the reserves ; a reduction is made for men serving at remote Asiatic posts; the War Office may send soldiers into the reserve before the end of their terms. Reduction is also made, from eleven to thirteen years and a half, for various degrees of educational acquirement. Exemptions are also made for family reasons and on account of peculiar occupation or profession. Individuals who personally manage their estates or direct their own commercial affairs (with the exception of venders of strong liquors) may have their entry into service postponed two years. Men are permitted to volunteer at seventeen (with consent of parents or guardians); all volunteers serve nine years in the reserve; those joining the Guards or cavalry must maintain themselves at their own expense. The total contingent demanded for army and navy in 1880 was 235,000, and 231,961 were enrolled ; of this deficit of 3,039, the greater number, 3,000, were Jews.

Organisation.|The Emperor is the Commander-in- Chief, who issues orders through the War Ministry, whose head is responsible for the general efficiency of the Army. There is also the " Imperial Head-quarters," under a general officer who, in the absence of the War Minister, takes the Emperor's orders and sees to their execution.The War Council, presided over by the War Minister, supervises all financial matters in connection with the army. There are also a High Court of Appeals, and the Headquarters Staff, who supervise the execution of all military duties. Commissariat, artillery, engineer, medical, military education, Cossack, and judge-advocate departments complete the list of bureaus.

The military forces are arranged into nineteen army corps: five comprise three divisions of infantry ; one, two divisions of cavalry; the remainder, two divisions of cavalry and one of infantry ; with a due proportion of light artillery and engineers the war strength of an army corps is 42,303 combatants, 10,755 horses, and 108 guns.

When war is declared an army is formed of two or more corps. The general commanding exercises supreme control, civil and military, if the force enters the enemy's country. His staff are detailed much as usual at an American army headquarters in the field.

There are in the active army|*Infantry:* 768 battalions (192 regiments, 48 divisions), 54 batt. riflemen. *Cavalry:* 56 regular regiments (4 cuirassiers, 2 uhlans, 2 hussars, 48 dragoons); 29 regt. Cossacks, divided into 20 divisions, kept in time of peace at 768 men (864 with sub-officers) per regiment. *Artillery :* 51 brigades, or 303 batteries of 8 guns each ; 30 horse-batteries of 6 guns each ; besides 14 batteries with Cossack divisions. Fifty "parks" and 20 sections of "parks" supply each infantry brigade and cavalry division with cartridges.

i2 2 5 Z. Oli*n'* S: HS o- Pi i H If if IRKESTllG H S'l 1O "I O 5rtG 13 3' H-y w jSu o . o F r H ta toS 5' oiSo ui 03g too P Wi- CO Ulo ,OtooVi 10oto 8114- Co CO O 04O 1f g CO 10JO COb)vQP COHI MToJj,f4Cjtna toCOCO CO COtoHI fe uiUig PIo-Itoto oblSP3Cj"1"to "to0Zjff.1Ln U o0310O 4IA 1Mtj M COOD4-H COJO0 MOJlo $"co a(5g.g,o$ UlUloO CO0 M HI a UlCO*Co* COHIo 10 O3 o 01 tO toc Ln M MO HIa M 4- CO3 0coCO COCOP M10 tn tnMCOCOS CO 4-,T PMM "o11M4 (1to$ to O o.0 OMJ4-w O -4 HI"51JJM& $ 10"coi toMI$ CON 8J uo 10O toVI4-1 OO313 OODM OsN n

jfl n

H C/l

During 1884 the engineer corps was reorganized. Henceforward the peace establishment will consist of seventeen battalions of sappers: eight battalions of pontoniers; sixteen field-telegraph companies, each of which is mounted, so as to maintain telegraphic communication for forty miles, and have two stations ; six engineering parks or trains, each ten sections, carrying each sufficient tools and material for an infantry division; four battalions of military railway engineers; four mine companies; two siege trains, and one telegraph instruction company. The whole is divided into six brigades, and provisions are taken for training recruits and supplying the losses during war. The fortress troops, for the defence of fortresses, consist of forty-three battalions of twelve hundred men each in time of war, and nine companies of three hundred men each. The depot troops, for garrison service, consist of thirteen battalions and three hundred detachments.

The reserve troops supply 204 battalions of infantry, 56 squadrons of cavalry, 57 batteries of artillery, and 34 companies of sappers. If mobilized, they are intended to supply 544 battalions, 56 squadrons, 144 batteries, and 34 companies of engineers. The second reserve, or " Zapas," consists of " cadres " for instruction, organized in time of war.

The training of the Russian infantry comprises that of skirmishing as of most importance ; the whistle is used to call attention; the touch is looser in the ranks than formerly ; squares to resist cavalry are no longer used; the Berdan breech-loader is the infantry arm; sergeant- majors wear officers' swords, and together with musicians carry revolvers.

A great stimulus has been given to rifle practice in the Russian army, with fair results, but complaint is made of want of good instructors. The dress and equipment of the infantry is noted for an absence of ornament, and hooks are substituted for buttons. Every thing has been made subordinate to comfort and convenience. Woollen or linen bandages are worn instead of socks. The entire outfit of the soldier weighs about fifty pounds. The Guards, alone, are yet permitted to wear their old uniform with buttons. The arms of the Turkestan troops are mixed Berdan and Bogdan rifles. The field clothing is generally linen blouse with cloth shoulder-straps, chamois-leather trousers, dyed red, and a white k$pi. Officers wear the same trousers in the field. Cossacks wear gray shirts of camel's hair.

The artillery is divided into field artillery and horse artillery, of which the strength is given elsewhere. The horse batteries have the steel four-pound gun.

Col. Lumley, of the British army, says: " In Russia it is believed that the field artillery is equal to that of any other Power, and the horse artillery superior." Lieut. Grierson, R. A., from his personal observation, confirms this opinion.

A British officer, who has had good opportunities, says the infantry drill is second to none.

It is not too much to say that, in any European conflict in the near future, the Russian cavalry will be conspicuous and extraordinarily effective. In a war with England, in

Asia, the use of large bodies of cavalry, organized, instructed, and equipped after the American plan, must become the main feature.

From the wonderful reforms instituted by Russia in her huge army of horsemen, which have put her before all other nations, not excepting Germany, we may expect to hear of wonderful mobility, stunning blows at the enemy's depots, and the appropriation of choice positions under his nose : of stubborn contests with the Anglo-Indian infantry, the only weapon a Berdan carbine; of communications destroyed by high explosives: especially, of the laying waste smiling Afghan valleys, inexpedient to occupy ;|these are a few of the surprises to which we may be treated if Russia gets the chance. In this manner she is doubtless prepared to take the initiative in her next war.

The bold operations of General Gourko in the Russo-Turkish war of 1878, afford the best illustration of the versatile qualities of the progressive military horseman since the American war, 1861-5. An Austrian officer says: "The Russian cavalry reconnoitred boldly and continuously, and gave proof of an initiative very remarkable. Every one knows that Russian dragoons are merely foot soldiers mounted, and only half horsemen: however, that it should come to such a point as making dragoons charge with the bayonet, such as took place July 16th near Twardista, seems strange. Cossacks and Hussars dismounted on the 30th, formed skirmishing lines, coming and going under the fire of infantry, protecting their battery, and conducting alone an infantry fight against the enemy. At Eski Zagra, July 3ist, the dragoons did not leave the field until all their cartridges were exhausted. On the other hand, the *offensive* action, and the spirit of enterprise and dash, which are the proper qualifications of cavalry, were not wanting in the Russians."

The whole of the regular cavalry of the line has been converted into dragoons armed with Berdan rifle and bayonet ; the Guard regiments must adopt the same change when ordered into the field, and the Cossacks have been deprived of the lance (excepting for the front rank); new musketry regulations have been prescribed. Great stress is now laid upon the training of both horses and men in the direction of long marches, and the passage of obstacles. Forced marches are also made to cover the greatest possible distances in the shortest possible time.

Swimming was practised in the Warsaw, Odessa, and Moscow districts, the horses being regularly taught with the aid of inflated bags tied under them. The Suprasl was crossed by the entire 4th Cavalry Division swimming. In order to acquire a thorough knowledge of pioneer duty, both the officers and non-commissioned officers of cavalry are attached to the engineer camp for a short course of instruction. In one division a regular pioneer squadron has been formed for telegraphic and heliographicduty. The mounted force, provided for in the Russian establishment, comprises twenty-one divisions of 3,503 sabres and 12 guns each, or an aggregate of 73,563 men and 252 field guns.

Among other experiments are noted that of 7 officers and 14 men of the Orenburg Cossacks who in November last in bad weather travelled 410 versts between Niji Novgorod and Moscow in 5 days|about 53 miles a day; then covering 685 versts from Moscow to St. Petersburg in 8 days| 56 miles a day ; on arrival an inspector reported horses fresh and ready for service ; the party was mentioned in orders, and presented to the Czar. A month before, in snow and intense cold, 7 officers and 7 men of the cavalry school covered 370 versts in 4 days|60 miles a day. It is asserted that the best Russian cavalry can travel 70 miles a day, continuously, without injury. General Gourko recently inspected two sotnias of Don Cossacks who had cleared 340 versts in 3 days, or 74 miles a day.

A feature of the Russian cavalry equipment is the pioneer outfit. consisting of tools for construction or destruction, as they desire to repair a bridge or destroy a railroad : this outfit for each squadron is carried on a pack-mule ; dynamite is carried in a cart with the ammunition train.

The Cossack (except of the Caucasus) is armed with a long lance (front rank only), a sabre without guard, and a Berdan rifle. Those of the Caucasus have in addition pistol and dagger, besides a *nagaska* or native whip. The uniform is blue, high boots, fur cap, cloak with cape. The snaffle-bit is universally used, even by the officers, although the average Russian troop-horse is noted for his hard mouth.

In the mounted drill of the Cossacks there is a charge as skirmishers (or " foragers ") called the " lava," which is executed at a great pace and with wild yells of " Hourra ! "

Lieut. Grierson, of the British army, writes that: " A big fine man mounted on a pony, with his body bent forward and looking very top-heavy, always at a gallop, and waving his enormous whip, the Cossack presents an almost ludicrous appearance to one accustomed to our stately troopers. But this feeling is dashed with regret that we possess no such soldiers."

Transport and Supply.|The Russian system of transport is in a very experimental and unsatisfactory state. It is the only army which provides regimentally for the *personnel* and *materiel* of this department. In each regiment is a non-combatant company, in which all.men required for duty without arms are mustered.

All military vehicles required for the regiment are under charge of this company. The intention of the system now developing is to reduce the quantity of transportation required. Besides the wagons and carts used for ordinary movements of troops, Russia will, in Afghanistan, depend upon the animals of the country for pack-trains and saddle purposes. After the *Camel,* of which large numbers exist in the region bordering Afghanistan on the north, the most important aid to Russian military mobility is the remarkable *Kirghiz Horse.* The accounts of the strength, speed, endurance, and agility of this little: animal are almost incredible, f but they are officially indorsed in many instances. He is found in Turkestan, and is more highly prized than any other breed. The Kirghiz horse is seldom more than fourteen hands, and, with the exception of its head, is fairly symmetrical; the legs are exceptionally fine, and the hoofs well formed and hard asiron. It is seldom shod, and with bare feet traverses the roughest country with the agility of a chamois, leaping across wide fissures on the rocks, climbing the steepest heights, or picking its way along mere sheep-tracks by the side of yawning precipices, or covering hundreds of versts through heavy sand, with a heavier rider, day after day. Its gaits are a rapid and graceful walk of five and one half to six miles an hour, and an amble at the maximum rate of a mile in two minutes. This animal crosses the most rapid streams not over three and one half feet deep, lined with slippery boulders, with ease. They are good weight carriers.f With a view of stimulating horse-breeding in Turkestan, the government in 1851 offered prizes for speed.J Kirghiz horses have been thoroughly tested in the Russian army. For modern cavalry and horse-artillery purposes they are unsurpassed. The average price is $6, but an ambler will bring $12. Great Britain is said to possess 2,800,000 horses, while Russia, in the Kirghiz steppes alone, possesses 4,000,000 saddle or quick-draught horses.

In 1878 the head-quarters baggage of the Grand Duke Nicholas required five hundred vehicles and fifteen hundred horses to transport it.

In 1869 a Russian detachment of five hundred men, mounted on Kirghiz horses, with one gun and two rocket-stands, traversed in one month one thousand miles in the Orenburg Steppe, and only lost three horses ; half of this march was in deep sand. In October, M. Nogak (a Russian officer) left his. detachment *en route,* and rode one horse into Irgiz, i66f miles in 34 hours.

The supply of the Russian army is carefully arranged under the central Intendance. The ration in the field was, in 1878, 14.3 ounces of meat, 14.9 black bread, preserved vegetables and tea, with an issue of brandy in the winter.Immense trains follow each division, at intervals, forming consecutive mobile magazines of food, A division provision train can carry ten days' supply for 230,030 men.

Moving both feet on a side almost simultaneously.

) The mounted messengers (pony express) over the steppes, use these horses, and carry with them, over stages of 350 miles in 8 days, an equipment and supplies for man and horse of nearly 300 pounds.

The greatest speed recorded (1853,) was 13 miles (on a measured course) in 27 minutes and 30 seconds.

Forage is now supplied for transport in compressed cakes, of which 20,000,000 were used by Russia in her last war.

Clothing is furnished by the supply bureau of certain regions in which there are large government factories; it is usual to keep on hand for an emergency 500,000 sets of uniform clothing.

Routes.|Having devoted a share of our limited space to an account of the roads leading to Herat from India, we may consider, briefly, certain approaches to Afghanistan or India from the northwest. This subject has been so clearly treated in a recent paper read before the Royal United Service Institution by Captain Holdich, R. E.,who surveyed the region referred to, in 1880, that we quote liberally as follows:

In improving our very imperfect acquaintance, both with the present military resources and position of Russia in Central Asia, and of the difficulties presented both geographically and by the national characteristics of the races that she would have to encounter in an advance south of the Oxus, a good deal has been already learned from the Afghans themselves. Among the turbulent tribes dwelling in and around Kabul, whose chief and keenest interest always lies in that which bears, more or less directly, on their chances of success in mere faction fights, which they seem to regard as the highest occupation in life, the Russian factor in the general game must be a matter of constant discussion. Thus it may possibly arise from their individual

A compressed ration of forage was extensively used by the Russians in 1878, weighing 3j pounds ; 5 days' supply could be carried on the saddle with ease.

interest in their national position that there is no better natural geographer in the world than the Afghan of the Kabul district. There is often an exactness about his method of imparting information (sometimes a careful little map drawn out with a pointed stick on the ground) which would strike one as altogether extraordinary, but for the reflection that this one accomplishment is probably the practical outcome of the education of half a lifetime.

Russia's bases of military operations towards India are two: one on the Caspian Sea at Krasnovodsk, and Chikishliar, with outposts at Chat and Kizil Arvat; and the other on the line of Khiva. Bokhara, Samarcand, and Margillan, which may roughly be said to represent the frontier held (together with a large extent of boundary south of Kuldja) by the Army of Tashkend, under General Kaufmann. But between this latter line and the Oxus, Russia is undoubtedly already the dominant Power. The mere fact of Russia having already thoroughly explored all these regions, gives her the key to their future disposal. There is no doubt that in all matters relating to the acquirement of geographical knowledge, where it bears on possible military operations, Russian perceptions are of the keenest. Her surveying energies appear to be always concentrated on that which yet lies beyond her reach, rather than in the completion of good maps to aid in the right government of that which has already been acquired.

With what lies north of the Oxus we can have very little to say or to do ;. therefore it matters the less that in reality we know very little about it. The Oxus is not a fordable river. At Khoja Saleh, which is the furthest point supposed to have been reached by the Aral flotilla, it is about half a mile wide, with a slow current. At Charjui it is about the same width, only rapid and deep. At Karki it is said to be one thousand yards wide, and at Kilif perhaps a quarter of a mile. But at all these places there are ferries, and there would be ample means of crossing an army corps, if we take into account both the Aral flotilla and the native material, in the shape of large flat-bottomed boats, capable of containing one hundred men each, used for ferrying purposes, of which there are said to be three hundred between Kilif and Hazarasp. These boats are drawn across the river by horses swimming with ropes attached to their manes. But under any circumstances it seems about as unlikely that any British force would oppose the passage of a Russian army across the Oxus as that it would interfere with the Russian occupation of the trans-Oxus districts ; but once south of the Oxus, many new conditions of opposition would come into play, arising principally from the very different national characteristics of the southern races to those farther north. It would no longer be a matter of pushing an advance through sandy and waterless deserts, or over wild and rugged mountains, difficulties which in themselves have never yet retarded the advance of a determined general, but there would be the reception that any Christian foe would almost certainly meet at the hands of a warlike and powerful people, who can unite with all the cohesion of religious fanaticism, backed up by something like military organization and a perfect acquaintance with the strategical conditions of their country. Most probably there would be no serious local opposition to the occupation by Russia of a line extending from Balkh eastwards through Khulm and Kunduz to Faizabad and Sar- hadd, all of which places can be reached without great difficulty from the Oxus, and are connected by excellent lateral road communications.

But the occupation of such a line could have but one possible object, which would be to conceal the actual line of further advance. Each of these places may be said to dominate a pass to India over the Hindoo Kush. Opposite Sarhadd is the Baroghil, leading either to Kashmir or to Mastuj and the Kunar valley. Faizabad commands the Nuksaa Pass. Khulm looks southwards to Ghozi and the Parwan Pass into Kohistan, while from Balkh two main routes diverge, one to Bamian and Kabul, the other to Maimana and Herat.

It would be a great mistake to suppose that this short list disposes of all the practicable passes over the Hindoo Kush. The range is a singularly well- defined one throughout its vast length ; but it is not by any means a range of startling peaks and magnificent altitudes. It is rather a chain of very elevated flattish-topped hills, spreading down in long spurs to the north and south, abounding in warm sheltered valleys and smiling corners, affording more or less pasture even in its highest parts, and traversed by countless paths. Many of these paths are followed by Kuchis in their annual migrations southward, with their families and household goods piled up in picturesque heaps on their hardy camels, or with large herds of sheep and goats, in search of fresh pasturage. South of the Hindoo Kush we find most of the eastern routes to our northwest frontier to converge in one point, very near to Jel- alabad. There are certain routes existing between the Russian frontier and India which pass altogether east of this point. There is one which can lie followed from Tashkend to Kashgar, and over the Karakoram range, and another which runs by the Terek Pass to Sarhadd, and thence over the Baroghil into Kashmir ; but these routes have justly, and by almost universal consent, been set aside as involving difficulties of such obvious magnitude that it would be unreasonable to suppose that any army under competent leadership could be committed to them. The same might surely be said of the route by the Nuksan Pass into the valley of Chitral and the Kunar, which

joins the Khyber route not far from Jelalabad. Its length and intricacy alone, independently of the intractable nature of the tribes which border it on either side, and of the fact that the Nuksan Pass is only open for half the year, would surely place it beyond the consideration of any general who aspired to invade India after accomplishing the feat of carrying an army through it. West of Kafirstan across the Hindoo Kush are, as we have said, passes innumerable, but only three which need be regarded as practicable for an advancing force, all the others more or less converging into these three. These are the Khak, the Kaoshan (or Parwan, also called Sar Alang), and the Irak. The Khak leads from Kunduz *via* Ghori and the valley of the Indarab to the head of the Panjshir valley. Its elevation is about thirteen thousand feet. It is described as an easy pass, probably practicable for wheeled artillery. The Panjshiris are Tajaks, and, like the Kohis- tanis generally, are most bigoted Suniu Mohammedans. The rich and highly cultivated valley which they inhabit forms a grand highway into Kohistan and Koh Dahman ; but all this land of terraced vineyards and orchards, watered by snow-cold streams from the picturesque gorges and mountain passes of the Hindoo Kush and Paghman mountains, |this very garden of Afghanistan, stretching away southwards to the gates of Kabul, is peopled by the same fierce and turbulent race who have ever given the best fighting men to the armies of the Amirs, and who have rendered the position of Kabul as the ruling capital of Afghanistan a matter of necessity ; with their instincts of religious hostility, it will probably be found that the Kohistani, rather than the Hindoo Kush, is the real barrier between the north and the south. The Sar Alang or Parwan Pass leads directly from Kunduz and Ghori to Charikar and Kabul. It is the direct military route between Afghan Turkestan and the seat of the Afghan Government, but is not much used for trade. It cannot be much over eleven thousand feet elevation, and it is known to be an easy pass, though somewhat destitute of fuel and forage. The next route of importance 1s that which leads from Balkh, *via* Bamian, to the Irak Pass on the Hindoo Kush, and into the upper watercourse of the Helmund River, and thence by the Unai over the Paghman range to Kabul. This is the great trade route from the markets of Turkestan and Central Asia generally to Kabul and India. The Irak, like the Parwan, is not nearly so high as has been generally assumed, while the Unai is a notoriously easy pass. This route is at present very much better known to the Russians, who have lately frequently traversed it, than to ourselves. Like the Parwan and the Khak, it is liable to be closed for three or four months of the year by snow. During the winter of 1879-80 they were open till late in December, and appear tobe again free from snow about the middle of April. Between these main passes innumerable tracks follow the " durras," or lines of watercourse, over the ridges of the Hindoo Kush and Paghman, which afford easy passage to men on foot and frequently also to " Kuchi " camels. These passes (so fat as we can learn) could, any of them, be readily made available for mountain artillery with a very small expenditure of constructive labor and engineering skill. In Koh Dahman nearly every village of importance lying at the foot of the eastern slopes of the Paghman (such as Beratse, Farza, Istalif, etc.) covers a practicable pass over the Paghman, which has its continuation across the Shoreband valley and over the ridge of the Hindoo Kush beyond it. But between the Khak Pass and the Irak, the various routes across the Hindoo Kush, whether regarded as routes to India or to Kandahar, although they by no means converge on Kabul City, must necessarily pass within striking distance of an army occupying Kabul. Such a force would have, first of all, thoroughly to secure its communication with the Oxus, and a strong position at Kabul itself.

Having the official statement of a military engineer with reference to the Oxus-Hindu-Kush line, as a barrier or base or curtain, we may pass to the principal approach to Herat from the northwest.

There are four distinct lines by which Russia could move on Herat:

I. From the *Caspian* base a trans-Caucasian army corps could move (only with the concurrence and alliance of Persia) by the Mashed route direct;

II. Or it could move outside Persian territory, from *Chikishliar* by the Bendessen Pass to Asterabad, and would then. have to pass through Persian territory to Sarakhs, or across the desert to Merv ;

III. From the *Tashkend-Bokhara* base a route exists *via* Charjui, the Oxus, direct to Merv ; and there is

IV. Also the well-known road by *Balkh* and Mamiana, direct to Herat.

Routes III. and IV. having just been discussed, let us look at Routes I. and II.

Referring to the small outline map of the trans-Caspian region, herewith, it will be seen that troops could embark from Odessa in the fleet of merchant steamers available, and, if not molested *en route* by hostile cruisers, would reach Batum in from 2 to 3 days, thence by rail to Baku in 24 hours, another 24 hours through the Caspian Sea to Krasnovodsk, a transfer in lighters to the landing at Michaelovsk, and the final rail transportation to the present terminus of the track beyond Kizil Arvat; this, it is said, will soon reach Askabad, 310 miles from Herat. The Secretary of the Royal Asiatic Society, Mr. Cust, with his wife, passed over this route in 1883, and testifies to the ease and comfort of the transit and to the great number of vessels engaged in the oil trade, which are available for military purposes, both on the Black and Caspian seas. He estimates that they could easily carry 8,000 men at a trip.

General Hamleyf says: "We may assume that if on the railway (single track) the very moderate number of 12 trains a day can run at the rate of 12 miles an hour, the journey would occupy 40 hours. The successive detachments would arrive, then, easily in two days at Sarakhs. A division may be conveyed, complete, in 36 trains. Thus, in six days a division would be assembled at Sarakhs ready to move on the advanced guard. An army corps, with all its equipments and departments, would be conveyed in 165 trains in 17 days. It would then be 200 miles|another 17 days' march|from Herat. Thus, adding a day for the crossing of the Caspian, the army corps from Baku would reach Herat in 35 days. Also the advance of a corps from Turkestan upon Kabul is even more practicable than before."

Mr. Cust says: " There are three classes of steamers on the Caspian.

1, the Imperial war steamers with which Russia keeps down piracy;

2, the steamers of the Caucasus and Mercury Company, very numerous and large vessels ; 3, petroleum vessels|each steamer with a capacity of 500 men.'

f Lecture before R. U. S. Institution (London), 1884.

The route from Tchikishliar *via* Asterabad (where it strikes the main Teheran-Mashed-Herat road) would be an important auxiliary to the railway line, *via* Asterabad. There is also a more direct caravan track running south of this across the Khorassan, from Asterabad (through Shahrud, Aliabad, Khaf, Gurian) to Herat; or, at Shahrud, an excellent road running between the two already described straight *(via* Sabzawar and Nishapar) to Mashed.

From Sarakhs to Merv the road is said to be good and fairly supplied with water. From Merv to Herat the well-worn expression " coach and four " has been used to denote the excellent condition of the road.f Yalatunis described as fertile, well populated, and unhealthy. From Penjdeh, where the river is sometimes fordable, the road follows the Khusk River, and, ascending the Koh-i- Baber Pass, descends into the Herat valley, immediately beneath it. f

In his plan of invasion, Skobeleff thought 50,000 men might undertake the enterprise without fear of disaster. This force could lje doubled from the Caucasus alone.

f For the first IOO miles the road follows the Murghab, which Abbott describes as " a deep stream of very pure water, about 60 feet in breadth, and flowing in a channel mired to the depth of 30 feet in the clay soil of the valley ; banks precipitous and fringed with lamarisk and a few reeds."

Band-i-Yalatun, or " bank which throws the waters of the Murghab into the canal of Yalatun."

f Before closing the chapter on the " Russian Forces," a brief description of the order of march customary in Central Asia may be proper. From a translation by Major Clarke, R. A., from Kotensko's " Turkestan," it appears that the horses accompanying Central Asian detachments are so considerable that the latter form, as it were, the escort of the former. As an Asiatic enemy nearly always attacks from every side, the distribution of the troops, during the march, must be such that they may be able to repulse the enemy no matter where he may appear. Usually, a half sotnia (70 men) of cavalry marches in advance at a distance from $ to ij miles, so as to be in view of main body. Immediately in front of main body marches a detachment of sappers and a company or two of infantry ; then part of the artillery ; then more infantry ; the train ; behind the train, remainder of artillery and infantry ; as a rear guard, a sotnia of cavalry. Bivouacs in the Steppe are usually chosen at wells, and are, in many respects, similar to those customary in the Indian country in America. First, an outer line of carts or wagons ; then the troops ; and inside, all the animals. The accompanying diagram is from *The jfourna! Royal United Service Institution* (London).

6

SECTION 6

V.
REVIEW OF THE MILITARY SITUATION.

THE purpose of this volume has been to give as much reliable information upon the cause of the Anglo-Russian dispute, the nature of the probable theatre of operations in case of war, and of the armies of the Powers concerned, as could be obtained and printed within a single fortnight. The richness of the available material made this especially difficult, comprising as it did the record of recent campaigns in Afghanistan, as well as the opinions of those who, like Vambery, Veniukoff, Rawlinson, Napier, and Cust, are authorities upon Asiatic topics.

As these lines are written the civilized nations of the world await with bated breath the next scene upon the Afghan stage.

Seldom when two gladiators, armed and stripped, enter the arena does a doubt exist as to their purpose. Yet such an exceptional uncertainty attends the presence of England and Russia on the border of Afghanistan.

At least 50,000 British soldiers are drawn up in front of the Indus awaiting a signal from their Queen. Nearly twice that number of Russian troops are massed on

April 18, 1885. 124

or near the northwestern angle of the Ameer's coun- try.

It is impossible to eliminate, altogether, from a study of the present military situation, certain political elements.

It is apparent that the Russians near Herat stand practically at " the forks of the road " ; it is a three-pronged fork|one branch running due south to the sea and two branches due east to India. The first-named requires but passing comment and only as it relates to Herat, planted on a route which cannot be controlled without its possession, for military and commercial reasons well understood.

As already explained, the routes to India, available to Russia, enable her to move from her base on the Merv- Herat line, both .*via* Balkh and Kabul, for the purpose of flanking a British column moving from Quetta westward, or of raiding the rich valley of the Helmund ; from Turkestan above this route, a British force moving from Kabul to Balkh could also be threatened. By the main Herat-Kandahar route an advance from the east could also be directly opposed ; the crossing of the Helmund by either army would probably be contested.

In case of war, whether Anglo-Russian or Russo-Af- ghan, the first great battle would doubtless be fought on the Kandahar-Ghazni-Kabul line.

Since the events noted in our first chapter (page 12) transpired, another page has been added to Afghanistan's blood-stained record. . After confronting each other on the Khusk River for some weeks a large Russian force under General Komaroff attacked (March 30, 1885) the Afghan troops at Penjdeh, and after a gallant resistance on the part of the native garrison it was utterly routed and the town occupied by the victors. The Russian casualties were inconsiderable, but the Afghans lost nearly 1,000 men.

General Hamley, the leading British military authority," shows that this line is, of all proposed, at once the most practicable and desirable line for the defence of India, f He says : " We should have a strong British governor in Kandahar, and a strong British force on the Helmund and on the road to Kabul; the railway completed to Kandahar, and, in case of a movement from Turkestan against Kabul, a force on our side on its way to occupy that city, and new recruiting grounds open to us amid warlike populations. Surely there can be no question as to which of these two sets of circumstances would give us most influence in Afghanistai, most power to oppose Russia and to maintain confidence in India."

The same authority approves Sir Michael Biddulph's recommendation to utilize the strong natural positions near Girishk on the Helmund. As to Afghanistan he testifies: "With a power like Russia closing on it, holding Persia and Persian resources subject to its will, it is in vain to think that Afghanistan will be long independent even in name. It is between hammer and anvil, or, to use a still more expressive metaphor, between the devil and the deep sea. Bound to us by no traditions, by no strong political influences such as might have been used to constrain them, the Afghan tribes, mercenary and perfidious to a proverb, an aggregate of tribes|not a nation,|will lose no time, when the moment occurs, in siding with the great power which promises most lavishly, or which can lay strongest hold on them."

Lieut.-General Sir. E. Hamley, K. C. B.

f Three lines had been considered : first, the line of the Eastern Sulimani, but this would leave the seaport of Kurrachee unprotected ; second, from Pishin northeast to Kabul.

J Gen. Hamley's remarks were made before the Royal United Service Institution (May 18, 1884), and, in the discussion which followed, Colonel Malleson said: "Recently in India some influential natives said to me: ' Russia will continue her advance ; she will not stop until she has gained the fertile country of Herat, and then she will intrigue with the native princes behind the Indus, and when you send an ar ny to meet her, you will find those native princes rising in your rear." I may fortify my own experience by what was told me by an Austrian gentleman w ho visited India about seven years ago. He paid a visit to the Maharaja, of Cashmere, who said to him : ' From you I hope to get the truth ; you are n)t an Englishman nor a Russian. Tell me which is the stronger|the Eng;:sh power or the Russian ; because it will be necessarily my duty, if Russia should advance, and if I should find Russia stronger than England, to go for the defence of my throne on the side of Russia. '"

The burning words with which General Hamley closed his lecture one year ago are singularly true to-day, and form a fitting termination to this sketch :

" I do not undervalue the many influences which will always oppose any policy entailing expense. But if the present question is found to be l. How shall we guard against a terrible menace to our Indian Empire? any cost to be incurred can hardly be admitted as a reason which ought to influence our course. Magnanimous trustfulness in the virtue and guilelessness of rival states; distrust and denunciation of all who would chill this inverted patriotism by words of warning; refusal of all measures demanding expense which do not promise a pecuniary return :|such is the kind of liberality of sentiment which may ruin great nations. The qualities of the lamb maybe very excellent qualities, but they are specially inapplicable to dealings with the wolf. Do those who shrink from expense think that the presence of Russia in Afghanistan will be inexpensive to us ? Will the weakness which will be the temptation and the opportunity of Russia be less costly than effectual defence? When we enter the councils of Europe to assert our most vital interests, shall we speak as we have been accustomed to speak, when our free action is fettered by the imminent perpetua menace to India? These are questions which, now put forth to this limited audience, will, perhaps, within the experience of most of us, be thundered in the ears of the nation. England is just now not without serious perplexities, but none are so fraught with possibilities of mischief as the storm which is now gathering on the Afghan frontier."

7

SECTION 7

LIST OF AUTHORITIES.1
    Anderson, Capt. "A Scheme for Increasing the Strength of the Native Armies," etc. f
    Army List, British Official, 1885.
    Biddulph, Gen. " The March from the Indus to the Helmund."
Bellew, II. W., C. S. I. "A New Afghan Question." f
Bengougii, Lieut-Col. " Mounted Infantry." f (From the Russian.)
Bisciioff, Major. " The Caucasus and its Significance to Russia." (Ger.) f
Bluxdell, Col. "British Military Power with Reference to War Abroad."
Baker, Col. " The Military Geography of Central Asia."
Colquhoun, Capt. " On the Development of the Resources of India in a

    Military Point of View." f
    Cantley, Major. " Reserves for the Indian Army." f
Callen, Major. " The Volunteer Force of India," etc. f
Cavenagh, Gen. " Our Indian Army."

Chapman, Lieut-Col. " The March from Kabul to Kandahar in 1880."
Clarke, Capt, " Recent Reforms in the Russian Army."
Cust, R., Sec. R. A. S. " The Russians on the Caspian and Black Seas."
Davidson, Major. "The Reasons why Difficulty is Experienced in Recruiting for the Native Army." f
Dalton, Capt. " Skobeleff's Instructions for the Reconnaisance and

Battle of Geok-Tepe." (From the French.)
Eli As, Capt. " A Streak of the Afghan War."
Esme-forbes, Lieut. " Cavalry Reform." f
Furse, Major. " Various Descriptions of Transport."
Gaisford, Capt. " NewModel Transport Cart for Ponies and Mules." f
Gloag, Col. " Military Reforms in India." f

Gowan, Major. " Progressive Advance of Russia in Central Asia." f
"The Army of Bokhara."! "Russian Military Manoeuvres in
the Province of Jaxartes." f (From the Russian.)
Graham, Col. " The Russian Army in 1882."

1 Unless otherwise designated, the authors named are officers of the British Army, and nearly all the works are in the Library of the Military Service Institution of the United States, (Governor's Island, N. Y. H.).
Journal Royal United Service /J/ /0 (London).
t *Journal of the United Service Institution of India* (Simla).
Gordon, Capt. " Bengal Cavalry in Egypt." f
Grierson, Lieut. " The Russian Cavalry,"f and " The Russian Mounted Troops in 1883." f
Greene, Capt. " Sketches of Army Life in Russia." (New York, 1881.)
Griffiths, Major. " The English Army." (London.)
Grey, Major. " Military Operations in Afghanistan."
Gerard, Capt. " Rough Notes on the Russian Army in 1876."
Goi.dsmid, Gen. "From Bamian to Sonmiani." "On Certain Roads

between Turkistan and India."
Hf.yland, Major. " Military Transport Required for Rapid Movements."
Holdich, Capt. " Between Russia and India."
Henneken, Gen. " Studies on the Probable Course and Result of a War

between Russia and England." f (From the Russian.) Hildyard, Lieut.-Col. " The Intendance, Transport, and Supply Service
in Continental Armies." Haskyns, Capt. " Notice of the Afghan Campaigns in 1879-81. From an
Engineer's View."

Hamley, Lieut.-Gen., Sir E. " Russia's Approaches to India." (1884.) Journal of the Military Service Institution of the United States.
Keltie, J. S. " The Statesman's Year-Book." (London, 1885.)
Kirchiiammer, A. "The Anglo-Afghan War."f (From the German.)
Kotensko. " The Horses and Camels of Central Asia." f " Turkestan."

(From the Russian.)
Little, Col. " Afghanistan and England in India." f (From the German.) Leverson, Lieut. " March of the Turkistan Detachment across the
Desert," etc. (From the Russian.)
Martin, Capt. " Tactics in the Afghan Campaign," f " Notes on the Operations in the Kurrum Valley."f " Horse-Breeding in Australia and India." f " Notes on the Management of Camels in the loth Company Sappers and Miners on Field Service." f " British Infantry in the Hills and Plains of India." f
Morgan, D. " A Visit to Kuldja, and the Russo-Chinese Frontier."
Morton, Capt. " Gourko's Raid." f (From the French.)
Mackenzie, Lieut.-Gen. " Storms and Sunshine of a Soldier's Life."
Mosa, P. " The Russian Campaign of 1879," etc. (From the Russian.)
Medley, Col. " The Defence of the Northwest Frontier." f
Newall, Lieut.-Col. " On the Strategic Value of Cashmere in Connection with the Defence of Our Northwest Frontier, "f
O'DoNOVAN, E. " The Merv Oasis." (New York, 1883.)
Price, Capt. " Notes on the Sikhs as Soldiers for Our Army." f

Pitt, Lieut. " A Transport Service for Asiatic Warfare," etc.
Ross, D., (Delhi Railway). " Transport by Rail of Troops, Horses, Guns, and War Materials." f
St. John, Major. " Persia : Its Physical Geography and People." f Strong, Capt. " The Education of Native Officers in the Indian Army.".). Steel, Veterinary-Surgeon. "Camels in Connection with the South Ai.
rican F.xpedilion, 1878-1879." f Shaw, Major. " Army Transport."
Sanderson, G. P. " The Elephant in Freedom and in Captivity."
Temple, Lieut. " An Historical Parallel|The Afghans and Mainotes."f
Tyrrell, Lieut.-Col. " The Races of the Madras Army." f
Trotter, Capt. " The Tribes of Turkistan." f
Trench, Col. " Cavalry in Modern War." (London, 1884.)
Upton, Gen. " The Annies of Asia and Europe." (New York, 1878.)
Veniukoff, Col. " The Progress of Russia in Central Asia." f (From the

Russian.)
Yaldwyn, Capt. " Notes on the Camel." f

INDEX.

Abazai, mil. post, 84

Abbaza, village, 100

Abdurrahman, the Ameer, 26, 55

Absuna, pass, 85

Abul-Khair, 2

Afghanistan:

Territory, 13, 16; mountains, 14; rivers, 14; roads, animals, 38-43; people, 16-25 ; army, 26-27 I cities, 28-36 ; military history, 43-55

Ahmed-Kheil, city, 79

Ahmed-Shah, 29

Akbar Khan, 47, 50

Akbar, the Great, 50

Akhurit Ziarut, city, 99

Akton Khel, city, 90

Alexander 1., 4

Alexander, Czar, 13

Al:xai:derof Macedon, 32

Ali Musjid, fort, 52, 64, 86

Altai, river, 3

Aliabad, 121

Amu Daria (Oxus), river, 13, 14

Aral, sea, 5, 116

Argandab, valley, 14, 32, 34, 99, 100

river, 99

Army, British :

Strength, 59; organization, 58; transport, 64; supply, 85 ; routes, 84 ; operations, 78

Indian: 62, 64

Army, Russian ;

Strength, 107 ; organization, 105 ; transport, 113 ; supply, 114 ; routes, 115

Aryan, race, i

Askabad, 120

Assin Killo, city, 88

Asterabad, 121

Atta Karez, mountain, 99, zoo

Attreck, river, 6

Auckland, Lord, 45

Aulicata, city, 5

Auran, mountain, 14

Aurangzeb, 50

Ayoub Khan, 82

B

Baber Khan, 13, 32

Baku, 120, 121

Balkash, mountain, 4

Balkh, city, 52, 117, 118, 119, 126

Bamian, pass, 36, 117

Baroghil, pass, 117

Barshor, valley, 96

Baru, military post, 84

Batum, 120

Bekovitch, Gen., 2

Beloochistan, state, 13, 91, 94

Bendessen, pass 119

Bengal, city, 46

Beratse, village, 119

Berlin, city, 9

Biddulph, Sir M., 53, 91, 98, 100, 12

Billigurungan, hills, 72

Bolan, pass, 46, 68, 94, 95

Bokhara, province, 6, 7, 9, 116, 119

Bombay, city, 46

Bori, valley, 20

Host, city, ioo

Broadfoot, Capt., aa

Browne, Gen., 53

Brydon, Dr., 48

Bunnoo, mil. post, 84

Burnes, agent, 46

Burrows, Gen., 55

Calmucks, 3

Camel, 38, 68, 113

Cashmere, Maharaja, 127

Caspian, sea, 2, 3, 5, 6, 116, 119, 120,121

Catharine II., 3

Cavagnari, Major, 13, 54

Ceylon, island, 72 Gimlari, mountain, 92

Chapman, Col., 77 Girishk, city, 14, 18, 41, 128

Charikar, town, 118 Gordon, Col., 64

Cliat, town, 116 Gourko, Gen., no, i1 1

Churjui, town, 116, 119 Graham, Sir L., 104

Chelmsfoul, Lord, 8 Green, Col., 66

Chemkent, city, 5 Grierson, Lieut., 109, 112

Chikishliar, town, 116, 119, 12i Guikok, range, 14

Chitral, town, 117 Gujrat, city, 52

Clarke, Major, 122 Guleir Surwandi, pass, 84

Conolly, M., 31 Gundamuck, city, 77, 88

Cossacks, 2 Gundana, town, 9

Gust, Mr., 120, 123 Gurian, city, 121

D H

Dadur, city, 66, 91, 94, 95 Haines, Sir F., 8

Dakka, city, 66, 70, 86 Hamley, Gen., 8, 9, 98, 120, 121,127, 128,

Dasht-i-Bedowlat, mountain, 94 I2Q

Delhi, city, 13, 43, 76 Har-i-Rnd, M, 54

Dera Ghazi Khan, village, 91 Hazaristan, river, 14

Dera Ismail Khan, city, 84, 91 Hazarasp, city, 116

Derajat, district, 92 Hazardarakht, mountain, 90

Djungaria, province, 2, 3 Hazarnao, city, 86, 88

Doaba, military post, 84 Helmund, river, 14, 15, 18, 55, 91, 99, too,

Dost, Mohammed, 31, 45, 46, 53 I18. ,.,7i ,38

Dozan, city, 68 Herat, city, 11, 12, 15, 18, 20, 24, 28, 29, 30,

E 3. 45. 53. 55, 84, 94,9s. 99. 100,115,117,

11o, 121, 126, 128 ; river, 14, 15, 30

Elephant, 70 ,

., , , Himalayas, mountain, 14

Ellenborough, Lord, 50 ... . . .

..,.. ' Hindu KOsh, mountain, 14, 15 18,31,36,

Elphmstone, Gen., 13, 27, 38, 47, 50, 88

. ,. , /ijtwat 115,117,118,110

Eski Zagra, town, 11o ,, ,', . T

HobhousD, SirJ.C.,45

F Hodjeni, province, 6

Faizabad, city, 117 Holdich, Capt., 113

Farrah, town, 14, 15, 100 Horse' yabQ' 4' i khirgiz, 113

Farza, village, 119

Fergana, province, 7

Ferrier, Gen., 28 Inderabad, river,

India, On the threshold of, 13

" Indus, river, 13, 18, 35, 46, 51, 65, 84, 91, 92

Gaisford, Capt., 103 Irak, pass, 118

Gayud Yara, plain, 96 Irgiz, fort, 4, 113

Geok Tep6, fort, 1 1 Irtish, river, 2, *3*

Genghiz Khan, 13, 29 Ispahan, city, 30

Ghazgar, valley, 20 Istalif, village, 119

Ghazni, city, 14,38,35,45,46,48,50, 84,91, .

96, 99, 117

Ghilzai, district, 96 Jacobadad, city, 66, 9a

Ghori, valley 118 Jagdallack, pass, 88

Gilan, province, 3 Jamrud, city, 17

Jelalabad, city, 14, 16, 34, 43, 48, 50, 66, 86,

1.8

Jizakh, province, 6

Jumrud, military post, 84, 85

K

Kabul, city, 9, 11, 14, 15, 16, 18, 31, 32, 33-36, 42, 45, 46, 50, 51, 52, 54, 55, 70, 77, 82, 84, 88, 90, 98, 101, 115, 117, 118, 119, 126, 127 ; river, 14, 31, 34, 66, 86

Kachi, plains, 92, 94

Kadani, plains, 96

Kafristan, province, 118

Kahriz, fort, 30

Kalat, city, 42

Kandahar, city, 14-16, 18, 31-35, 41, 42, 45, 46, 48, 52, 55, 70, 82, 84, 91, 94, 95, 98, 99, 101, 126, 127

Karakoran, mountain, 117

Karkacha, pass, 88

Karki, town, 116

Kash, river, 14, 15 ; city, 15

Kashgar, 117

Kashmir, city, 117

Kaufmann, Gen., 7, 9, 11, 53,116

Kelat, town, 16, 94, 95

Khaiber, pass, 34, 36, 50, 84, 85,88, riS

Khanikoff, M., 29

Khaf, 121

Khak, pass, 44, 118, 119

Khinar, pass, 88

Khiva, province, 5, 6, 7, 116

Khuja-Saleh, city, 116

Khokand, province, 5, 6, 7

Khoja-Amran, mountain ridge, 96, 98

Khorassan, province, 4, 13, 94, 98, 121

Khulm,city, 117

Khurd-Kabul, pass, 47, 48, 88

Khurd-Khaiber, pass, 86

Khusk', river, 122

Khirtar, mountain, 94

Kilif, city, iz6

Kizil Arvat, city, 116, 120

Koh Daman, mountain, 118,119

Kohut, rail, post, 84

Kohistan, province, 117,118

Koh-i-Baber, mountain, 122

Kokiran, district, 99

Komaroff, Gen., 126

Kotensko, 122

Krasnovodsk, city, 6, 116, 120

Kuh-i-Baba, mountain, 30

Kujlak-Kekur, valley, 96

Kuldja, city, 116, 120

Kunar valley, 117

Kunduz, city, 117, 118

Kurrachee, city, 76, 127

Kuram, river, 14 ; valley, 70, 79,90; fort, 90

Kusmore, village, 92

Kussun, fort, 30

Lalaberg, valley, 86

Lalgoshi, village, 91

Lahore, city, 35, 46, 76

Landi Khana, village, 86

La.Ii Jowain, city, 15, 100

Likharcff, Gen., 2

Logar, valley, 90

London, city, 1 1

Lora, river, 96

Lumsdcn, Sir P., 12, 26

Lumley, Col., 109

M

Mackenzie, Gen. C., 27

Mackeson, fort, 84

McNaghten, Sir W., 47, 50

Mahmoud, sultan, 13, 45

Mahomet, i

Mahommed Azim, 90

Maimana, town, 117, 119

Malleson, Col., 8, 127

Malta, 74

Margilan, town, 116

Maris, tribe, 94

Martin, Lieut., 41, 77, 79, 80

Marvin, C., 8

Mashed, city, 121

Mastuj, town, 117

Maude, Gen., 53

Mazanderan, province, 2

McCleltan, saddle, 73

Merv, province, u, 12, Iiq, 1ai, 126

Michaelovsk, town, 120

Michni, fort, 84

Mithunkot, town, 91

Mogul, 32

Mooktur valley.

Mooltan, city, 91

Moscow, city, 11, 48, i1 1

MDlla, pass, 94

Munro, fort, 93

Murchat, town, 18

Murghab, river, 35,121

Mysore, province, 72

N

Nadir, Shah, 43, 50

Nahur, Maharajah of, 70

Napier, Lord, 8, 123

Napoleon, 4, 44

Nicholas, Grand Duke, 113

Nijni Novgorod, town, i1 1
Nishuper, townl

Nogak, M., 113

Nott, Gen., 48

Nuksan, pass, 117,118

O

Odessa, city, i11, 120

O'Donovan, M., 24

Orenburg, province, 3, 4, 5

Orloff, Gen.,4

Outram, Capt., 42

Oxus, (See Amer. Daria)

P

Paghman, mountains, 118, 119

Panjshir, valley, 118

Panjwai, town, 99

Paropismus, mountains, 30

Parwan, pass, 117, 118

Pat, clay, 92

Paul, Emperor, 3

Peiwar, pass, 84, 90

Pekin, 69

Penjdeh, town, 122, 126

Persia, 2, 6, 7, 30, 43, 44

Perwan, pass, 46,

Perovsky, fort, 5

Peter the Great, 2

Petropanlovsk, province, 3

Peshawur, city, 34, 35, 44, 45, 50, 84

Pishin, village, 91, 96 ; plain, 96, 98, 137

Pollock, Gen., 50, 51

Pottinger, Major, 29

Primrose, Gen., 53, 55

Q

Quetta, city, 76, 84, 91, 94, 95, 96, 98, 126

Raganpur, city, 91

Rawlinson, Sir II., 8, 28, 51, 124

Roberts, Gen., 10, 53, 54, 55, 79, 82, 90, 1or

Rogan, village, 91

Ross, railway manager, 74, 76

Rudbar, town, 100

Russian Army : strength, 107 ; organization, 105, 112; transport, 113, 115; supply, 114; routes, 115, 123

Sabzawar, city, 15, 121

Sale, Sir R., 34, 38

Samarcand, city, 7, 11, 30, 116

Samson, 22

San Stefano, 104

Sarahks, town, 12, 30. 120, 121

Sargo, pass, 84, 90

Sarhadd, town, 117

Saunders, Major, 29

Scinde, province, 46, 91

Seistan, district, 14,15

Shahrud, town, 121

Shere Ali, 52

Shikapur, town, 46

Shul Kadar, fort, 84

Shurtargurdan, pass, 84, 90

Singh Runjit, 45

SirpQl, town, 18

Skobeleff, Gen., It, 101, 121

Stewart, Sir D., 42, 53, 101

Stolietoff, Gen., 10

St. Petersburg, 3, in

Sufed Koh, mountain, 14, 88

Sujah Shah, 44, 45, 46

Sulimani, mountains, 127

Suprasl, river, i1 1

Surkh Denkor, 86

Surkhab river, 88

Takwir, mountain, 92

Taktipul, town, 99

Targai, fort, 4

Tartar a, pass, 85

Tashkend, city, 5, 55, 116, 117, 119

Teheran, 121

Tehernayeff, Gen., j, 6

Tejend, river, 12

Temple, Sir R., 68 Vernoye, fort, 5

Terek, pass, 117 Volga, river, 3

Timwi, 13, 29, 50 W

Trench, Col., 102 Warsaw, city, i1 1

Troitsk, province, 3 Washir, town, 100

Turkestan, *g, 30, 36,* 43, 113, "5. 1. I27 Wolseley, Lord, 69, 101

Turnak, valley, 14

Twarditsa, town, 1 1o

Yakoub, Khan, 54, 55

1 Yalatun, town, 122

TJnai, river, 118 Yaldwin, Capt., 38, 41

Ural, mountains, 3, 4 Yaxartes, river, 4, 5

V Z

Vamb6ry, M., 24, 31, 4 Zurmat, district, 22

Veniukoff, M., 4, 5, 6, 7, "4 Zohak, fort, 36

"./. .
'"". ' ,...'?! .VV."V" '
LlaOW rVJ.E2i.
-.... :.....
.I- . .!IMPORTANT STANDARD WORKS
RECENTLY PUBLISHED.

PRE-HISTORIC AMERICA. By the Marquis Be Nadaillac, translated by N. D'ANVERS, author of "A History of Art." Edited with notes by V. H. Dall. Large 8vo, with 219 illustrations $5 oo

Chief Contents.|Man and the Mastodon, The Kjokkemmoddings and Cave Relics, Mound Builders, Pottery, Cliff Dwellers, Central American Ruins, Peru, Early Races, Origin of American Aborigines, etc., etc.

THE DISCOVERIES OF AMERICA TO THE YEAR 1525. By Arthur James Weise. Second edition. One large octavo volume, with maps $4 50

The work presents the most important and veritable information of what was known by the ancients respecting the continent and islands in the Western Hemisphere, together with that found in the Sagas of Iceland and Greenland in relation to the discoveries of the Northmen, and also that contained in certain rare books, manuscripts, and maps, descriptive of the explorations of Columbus, the Cabots, Cortereal, Verrazzano, and other navigators, to the year 1525

A HISTORY OF THE THIRTY YEARS' WAR. By Anton
Gindely, Professor of German History in the University of Prague. Translated by Andrew Ten Brook, recently Professor of Mental Philosophy in the University of Michigan. Second edition. Two volumes, octavo, with maps and illustrations . . . $4 oo

LIFE AND TIMES OF GUSTAVUS ADOLPHUS. By the
Hon. John L. Stevens, LL.D., recently United States Minister to Stockholm. 8vo, with new portrait engraved on steel . $2 50

THE COMPLETE WORKS OF ALEXANDER HAMILTON.RECENT TRAVEL AND DESCRIPTION.

Including his Contributions to the " Federalist." Edited, with introduction and notes, by Henry Cabot Lodge. Seven volumes, handsomely printed from type, with two portraits engraved on steel. *Edition limited to $x copies.* . . . . $35 oo

CONTENTS.

I. Revolutionary. Government and the V. Foreign Relations.

Constitution. VI. The Excise and Whiskey Rebellion.
II. Taxation and Finance. Miscellaneous.
III. National Banks. Coinage, Industry, VII. Miscellaneous.
and Commerce. VIII. Private Correspondence.
IV. Foreign Relations. IX. The Federalist.
G. P. PUTNAM'S SONS, New York and London.$1.75

The Mt-rv Oasis : Travels and Adventures East of the Caspian during the Years 1879-'80-81, Including Five Months' Residence in the Tekk$ Territory. By $. O'DoN-Ovan, correspondent of the *London Daily News.* With portrait, maps, and fac.similes of diplomatic documents. 2 volumes, large octavo, $7.

' He tells his story with the ready pen of an experienced writer, and though his book is a large one it has no dull pages.1 |*Pn.ss,* Phila.

" His style is extremely vivid and picturesque, his anecdotes are many and varied, and his portraits of Turcomans and Persians are graphic and life-like to the last degree. Altogether, the book will fulfil even the high expectations which have been naturally raised by the letters to the *Daily News"*|*Pall .Mall Gazette,* London.

" Mr. O'Donovan's visit single-handed to the Tekke" stronghold during a time of wild excitement is an instance of daring to which we are precluded from applying the harsh term 'fool-hardiness' by the excellence of the present book."|*Atkeneeum,* London.

Six Months in Persia. By Edward Stack. 2 volumes, octavo, with
seven elaborate maps, $4.50.

11 A welcome addition to our knowledge of this interesting but almost unknown land."|*Christian Union.*

Italian Rambles. By James Jackson Jarves, author of "The Art
Idea," " Italian Sights," etc. i6mo, cloth extra, $1.25. Cuban Sketches. By James W. Steele. Octavo, cloth extra, $1.50. " The book gives a well-written tale of topics which are of interest both to tourist and to those who enjoy travelling at their own firesides."|*Christian Register.*

MISS ISABELLA BIRD'S TRAVELS.

Unbeaten Tracks in Japan. By Isabella Bird. Library edition, 2 volumes, octavo, fully illustrated, $5.00. Popular edition, i volume, octavo, fully illustrated, $3.00.

" Beyond question the most valuable and the most interesting of recent books concerning Japanese travel. One of the most profitable of recent travel records. |*Eveniug Post.*

A Lady's Life in the Rocky Mountains. 121110, cloth, illustrated,

11 Her whole experience is a singular combination of the natural and the dramatic, as well as the most encouraging record of feminine confidence and masculine chivalrous- ness."|*Spectator.*

Six Months Among the Palm Groves, Coral Reefs, and Volcanoes of ths Sandwich Islands. Octavo, cloth, illustrated, $2.50. " Miss Bird is the ideal Traveller."| *London Spectator.*

The Golden Chersonese, and the Way Thither. Octavo, cloth, with 24 illustrations, and 2 maps, $2.25.

Sketches of travel in the Malayan Peninsula.

" There never was a more perfect traveller than Miss Bird. Interesting extracts could be made from every page of the book one of the cleverest books of travel of the year."|*New York Times.*

G. P. PUTNAM'S SONS, 27 & 29 West 23d St., New York. 18 Henrietta Street, Covent Garden, London.

A HISTORY OF THE THIRTY YEARS' WAR. By Anton Gindely, Professor of German History in the University of Prague. Translated by ANDREW Ten Brook, recently Professor of Mental Philosophy in the University of Michigan. Second Edition. Two volumes, octavo, with maps and illustrations . . . $4 oo

This most important period of European History, .1 right understanding of which is essential to the proper comprehension of Europe to-day, has long waited for an historian. The work of 13chiller, while thoroughly readable, was written vithout any special historical preparation, and at n. ti.ne v. hen the collections of government archives were not accessible. The little handbook of Gardiner is a most admirable summary, but is too condensed for general reading. It is believed that the present work, which has been prepared by an historian of the highest position and authority, and while thoroughly trustworthy for the purposes of the scholar, is full of interest for the general reader, will meet all the requirements, and will remain the authority on the subject.

11 May safely be pronounced better than the best."|*Dis. of Christ,* Cincinnati.

u His portraitures are vividly drawn, and his battle scenes are pictured with great realistic power."|*Zion's Herald.*

" The clear style of the translation makes the reading of the book not only easy but delightful."|*Bulletin,* Philadelphia.

u The translator has not only performed his task in a masterly manner, but by his presentation of this admirable work to English readers, has placed them under a debt of obligation."|*Portland Press.*

u Prof. Gindely has achieved true success in the historical line ; he has a real genius for such labors."|*Post,* Hartford.

't Wonderfully well drawn."|*Advocate,* Cincinnati.

" It will doubtless take its place at once as the work of standard authority on the subject."|*Critic and Good Literature.*

'" Leyond all question the best history of the Thirty Years' War yet published." |*Phila. Item.*

u Indispensable to the student, For the general reader it is one of the most picturesque in history."|*Hartford Courant.*

" Unquestionably the best history of the Thirty Years' War that has ever been written."|*Baltimore A tnerican.*

u Must take a high and permanent place in historical literature."|*Brooklyn Eagle.*

11 It is not the least of the services to the cause of right thinking that has at last given us a history of this period which bids fair to bring the two lines (scholarly and popular thought) together.

u It would be hard to name among recent works a more overwhelming indictment of the policy and methods of imperial Jesuitry|a more satisfactory statement of what the Roman Papacy owes to the art and devotion of the Society of Jesus ; nor, we may add, a more thorough exposure of the Macaulay romance, that the Reformation in its spread followed the Saxon and Northern races, and proved unacceptable to people of Romanic descent. '|*N. Y. Independent.*

" He writes wfth the calmness of a philosopher and the correctness of a scholar, and the work will take rank with the best histories of modern times."|*Harrisburg Telegram.*

PROSE MASTERPIECES FROM MODERN ESSAYISTS : comprising single specimen essays from Irving, Leigh Hunt, Lamb, De Quincey, Landor, Sydney Smith, Thackeray, Emerson, Arnold, Morley, Helps, Kingsley, Ruskin, Lowell, Carlyle, Macaulay, Froude, Freeman, Gladstone, Newman, Leslie Stephen. These essays have been selected with reference to presenting specimens of the method of thought and the literary style of their several writers, and also for the purpose of putting into convenient shape fur direct comparison the treatment given by such writers to similar subjects.

The Mutability op Literature, by
Irving.
The Wokld Of Books, by Hunt.
Imperfect Sympathies, by Lamb.
Conversation, by Dc O,uincey.
Petition Of Thk Tnut;s, by Landor.
Benefits up Parliament, by Landor.
Fallacies, by Smith.
Nn. Nisi Bonum, by Thackeray.
Compe

Isi Bonum, by Thacker
Nsation, by Emerson.

My Winter Garden, by Kingsley.
Work, by Ruskin.
On A Certain Condescension In For-
Eigneks, by Lowell.
On Histoky, by Carlyle.
History, by Macaulay.
The Science Of History, by Froude.
Race And Language, by Freeman.
Kin Beyond The Sea, by Gladstone.
Private Judgment, by Newman.
An Apology For Plain Speaking, by

Stephen.
s And Light, by Arnold. Popular Culture, by Morley. Art Of Living With Others, by Helps.

3 vols., 16mo, bevelled boards, with frontispieces on steel, gilt tcp, in box, each $1 25

The set in extra cloth, with cloth box 4 50

The same in Russia-leather binding and case, round corners, red edges 10 00

The same, large paper edition, with portraits, cloth extra, gilt top, rough edges 7 50

THE ESSAYS OF ELIA. By Charles Lamb. "The Temple Edition,." Handsomely printed on laid paper from new type, with etchings by James D. Smillie, F. S. Church, R. Swain Gifford, and Charles A. Platt. Octavo, cloth extra. *About* .... $4 oo

The same, Islington Edition, 250 copies only, with proof impression of etchings *on satin.* Quarto, *numbered,* printed upon pure linen paper ; cloth, uncut .... $10 oo

AUTHORS AND PUBLISHERS; A MANUAL OF SUGGESTIONS FOR BEGINNERS IN LITERATURE : comprising a description of publishing methods and arrangements, directions for the preparation of MSS. for the press, explanations of the details of book-manufacturing, with instructions for proof-reading, and specimens of typography, the text of the United States Copyright Law and information concerning International Copyrights, together with general hints for authors. Octavo, cloth extra .... $i oo

l Full of valuable information for authors and writers. A most instructive nd excellent manual."|*Harper's Monthly* (Easy Chair).

G. P. PUTNAM'S SONS, PUBLISHERS,
NEW YORK AND LONDON. Js
DEC 18 1941